Vibes and Feelings:
THE FEELINGS

VERNON PADDY

authorHOUSE®

AuthorHouse™
1663 Liberty Drive
Bloomington, IN 47403
www.authorhouse.com
Phone: 833-262-8899

Published by AuthorHouse 03/25/2021

ISBN: 978-1-6655-2108-6 (sc)
ISBN: 978-1-6655-2112-3 (e)

Library of Congress Control Number: 2021906345

Print information available on the last page.

Contents

2 Types of Justice

America with its 2 types of justice
One you have to die
One that shows them up, for all their lies
No parts of it is right
You start to guess who dies?
Whose justice shows us their lies?
It cut clear and dry
Black and White
2 types of justice one for them
The other for us
Rosa refused to sit at the back of the buss
Martin died marching for us
Bob sing it in his songs of freedom
They quiet up Malcolm X
You knew what was coming next
2 types of justice set in stone
Stem from envy and hate
It's the main cause of so many broken homes
Mothers cry, Fathers die
Millions have marched and protest over the years
They take a little break
They ease up
To avoid the bad press
You can bet it's a Black man that will die next
2 types of justice we have never seen equality
Don't get this mixed up
This America is totally screwed up
Their broken system built on hate, lies and greed
We will never truly clean up the blood stains from these streets
The place reek, it smell stink
They signed the deals with dirty ink
The whole of America's history stink

From start till now
A so-so rip and rob
A so-so promises and lies
A so-so cut clear and dry
Black vs White
Years they've been planning to wipe out the Black race
Their female spoil their plans
Mix up mix up and start the new Black man
America new problem, the people they hate
Is now a part of their generation
Wait!
This started way back in slavery
When master couldn't keep his eyes of big mama sexy
They still hate us no matter our shade
They refused to accept us back then
Master was the reason we carried their DNA
2 types of justice America it's a shame
From the backs of Blacks
From slavery
You all gain your fortune and fame
From the backs of Blacks
From slavery
America became this land filled with blood sweat and tears
With their 2 types of justice
None of it is fair

50 Humans Sacrificed

"For the victims of the Orlando shooting"

50 humans sacrificed
Fifty humans lost their lives
Why is this world filled with such hate?
Oh it's a disgrace
When will mankind realize
each man uniqueness is the heavenly Father's design?
When we see souls
not color, race or other's choices
this world will be nicer, a whole lot quieter

50 humans sacrificed
Fifty humans lost their lives
There are no words to express such emptiness
such a lost
This world needs peace not wars
Mankind needs to open their eyes
realize we all can coexist
mingle and mix
enjoying of this earth to the fullest
Living our lives till the Father calls it
I'm tired to read about senseless killings like this
Guns is an invention
It's men and their intentions
their evil plans
Their messed up minds
There are those with cruel intentions
their hearts are so dark
it goes with their sick thoughts

Please don't trust any shadow after dark
careful how you talk
watch your steps while you walk

50 human sacrificed
Fifty beautiful humans lost their lives
We will never truly know the why
Let's hold our love ones close at all times
Keeping memories alive
Sleep well, rest in peace 50 beautiful souls

2020

Fair is fair
Just let me get my equal share
Find your own inner peace
Just give us justice
Wake up!
Are you blind!
You don't see how the system is disgusting
How it's one sided
It curry favor
It carry the wrong flavor
Wake up!
Are you blind!
You don't see how they are killing our Black backsides
Fair is fair
Just let me get my equal share
We need Moses laws
Eye for an eye
You don't see what's going on in all walks of society
You blind!
Things and time only rewind
We are seeing the same old crimes
Wait! Wait!
You think a just now they have been killing Blacks
No
We have always made a fuss
Just is just
Such is such
The system stink
The system set away
It no balance
It no level
Fair is fair
Just let me get my equal share

2021 Virus Free

2021 me a beg you
Me a beg you
Me a plea
Come in clear and clean
Virus Free
2021 me a beg you
Me a beg you
Me a plea
Be a better year for all of we
2021 me a beg you
Me a beg you
Me a beg you
Come in slow and steady
Drama free
No type of hype
Have a heart
Look out for we
We been through the fire
2020 was hell on earth
To blouse and skirt
2021 me a beg you
Me a beg you
Me a plea
Come in nice and easy
Give us a chance to warm up
A chance to clear our heads
Last year was dread
Red, red, red
Blood stain red
2021 me a beg you
Me a beg you
Me a plea

Come in humble
Have a heart for we
We suffer enough
Last year was ruff
Covid-19 kill nuff
The struggle was real
We hardly made ends meet
Some of us still on shaky feet
2021 me a beg you
Me a beg you
Me a plea
I am the spokesman for all of us
Hear me out
No me not shouting
My volume is just up
For we all stress out nuff, nuff
Come and gently ease in
Clear and clean
Most important
Virus free
2021 I know you hear me
I know you can see
The countless suffering 2020 have done to all of we
So this is my plea
Me a beg you
Me a beg you
Take is easy on we

A Change

The wind has changed
I now have to adjust my sail
Or be swept away
There is a shift in the tide
Low, I'm about to be grounded
I need a new route
A new start, a do over
Fresh beginning
I've been right here before
Starting all over again, it was rough
Many sleepless nights, tears flowed
My mind rewinds, fast forwards, replaying life
Life in past time, its been done, I did it
Was it the right way?
Then why am I on the high way?
Why am I the one?
Why! Why! Why!
I need a lucky star, I need a break
Life is a give and take
You win some, you lose some
It's never fun being on the short end of the stick
Am I being punished, over your rubbish?
Was I too quick to split?
The going did get tough
I stood my ground the best I could
It seems you got great pleasure, from seeing my pain
Replacing me as if it were a game
I saw right through you, seeking fortune and fame
It was a little too late
I was already out the gate
This is my faith
My heart is filled with love still, never hate

A few regrets
I'm going to correct the mistakes
I'm going to hold my head high
move forward, think positive
I might be the winner yet
I might see the rainbow again
I might even love again

A Flow

The writing has been on the wall
A few years I've been standing tall
With all the evil forces that surround me
All the negative vibes
I stand my ground
Never have I changed my route
I spoke my mind
Praising Jah all the time
I found my voice
Years ago when I sight Rasta light
Rasta lifestyles
Rasta truth
Rasta rights
I and Jah began a relationship
I found the strength to tap into my inner and outer vibes
For Rasta represents a clear vibes
Rasta is pure peace
Planting spiritual food for the World to eat
The mighty Herb open all doors to longer and stronger living
You don't see how government oppose
Always trying to kill it before it grows
I say let it grow as your locks grows
As your Rass flows lets the sweet aroma blows
Smoke and hold humble thoughts
You and Jah will never part
Remember Jah is always a part of your heart

A New Being

By: Mia Atre & Vernon Paddy

From nothing to something
From least to most
From broken to mend
From enemy to friend
From friends to lovers
From hidden to revealed
From secret to confession
From an idea in my head, now words to be read
From nothing to something
From start to end
From old to new
From me to you
From you to I
From conception to birth
A new being
From in to out
From oneness to togetherness
From single to double
From thoughts in my head
From pen to paper
Words, sound and power
From nothing to something
From fire to ice
From sour to sweet
From far to near
From hate to love
From being lonely to be comforted
From sunrise to sunset
From worries to a clear mind set
From you to I

From me to you
A new being
From dark to clear
From wrong to right
From war to peace
From drought to rain
From a seed to a plant
From being hungry to be fed
From sickness to health
From living to death
A new being

A New Song

Everyday a child is born
Everyday a soul is gone
Life recycles
Young for old
Everyday a new light is turned on
Everyday an old light is turned off
Life recycles
New for worn
Young for grown
Life recycles

I hear the music in my head
Guess I'm alive not dead
I hear the ticking of my heart
Jah love for me will never depart
I claim more life in Jah name
I give nothing but praises everyday
This new song I sing
With Jah I got everything
Joy filled my soul
I shall live with Jah forever more

Everyday we get a chance to start anew
Leaving behind the old
Everyday deserve its worth of praises
Each day is filled with its own woes
Yesterday has come and gone
Today will bring its own joy and sorrow
Live with less regrets
Give your more to receive your less
Love Jah more never less
As we grow we'll know how to appreciate what we get
Always give thanks endless

———

A Prayer

Jah give me more fruitful days
Reserve a piece of Mount Zion for I
Give me healing of my mind and body
Lead me, oh Jah
I will follow humbly
Ever respecting Mother Nature and Father Time
Let people see I as a child of the great King
Let me reap my rewards in your Holy Kingdom
Oh Jah Jah
As I trod Earth be by my side
Oh Jah Jah
Let I be up full and do the right things
Oh Jah Jah
Let me continue to love you
Oh Jah Jah
Keep my hands clean and my heart with pure thoughts
Oh Jah Jah
Let my deeds toward my fellow men be respectful
Oh Jah Jah
Let clean words flow from my mouth
Oh Jah Jah
Let you be my inspiration only
Oh Jah Jah
Bring me uplifting meditations
Oh Jah Jah
Let me reach high higher heights
Oh Jah Jah
This I pray
Oh Jah Jah

A Tree

Today I plant a tree
Hoping that one day it will bear fruits
From my labor I can feed myself and my neighbors
It's a flow through Mother Nature
Today I plant a tree
It gave me great pleasure, from such hard labor
We will reap from what we sow
Just plant a tree and watch it grow
It's a vibes through Mother Nature
With Father Time we'll eat come next season
Today I plant a tree
Praises to the all Mighty Creator
This Earth he gave
Knowledge to man to cultivate
Just watch and wait, we'll enjoy of this fruit
Hopefully when I'm recycled, made a new and is gone
This new generation will continue to cultivate
Planting more trees
So they too can eat of their labor

A Vibes

I met a girl
She was the lighter shade of black
So she thought she was all that
When she open her mouth to chat
It was pure crap that came out of her trap
She had the weirdest set of tired eyes
Like she wasn't sleeping well at night
Her body looked overload
As if spending too much time a road
She had a nice pair of tits that I must admit
I spent the rest of the night reminiscing
What's this girl missing?
What would make her tick?
Was her mind sane or sick?
Would she be a bundle of fun to be with?
She work the room like a pro
It showed she knew what she was doing
She now became very intriguing
Got me so excited
Her story I knew was worth writing
I just wish she wouldn't speak
It was so frightening
How could such a pretty face be such a waste?

Africa is Calling

Africa is calling, calling, calling your names
Africa is calling, calling, calling
don't pretend like you don't hear
Open up your ears
A beg you all to obey
Africa is calling, calling, calling your names
Africa is calling, calling, calling
don't act like you don't care
The lack of knowledge is a fear
Brothers and sisters re-educate your minds
know the truth from all the lies
then and only then we can soar to new heights
Africa is calling, calling, calling your names
Africa is calling, calling, calling
Brothers and sisters don't be afraid
Get to know Jah
the knowledge of Jah brings inner peace every time
you will praise Jah for the rest of your days
love, peace and harmony is all we should share
Africa is calling, calling, calling your names
Africa is calling, calling, calling
It's time for another Exodus
Movement of Jah people
Time to leave out of Babylon
It's time to live a Zion
Don't hesitate you might be too late
Only the chosen few shall enter Zion gate
Africa is calling, calling, calling out our names
Africa is calling, calling, calling out our names
Africa is calling, calling, calling
let's all prepare for this physical and mental journey

Africa is Calling

Africa is calling, calling, calling my name
Africa is calling, calling, calling my name
Take me down to Africa
With its rich African soil
Let me plant up the herb
Praising Jah all the time
Africa is calling, calling, calling my name
Africa is calling, calling, calling my name
Take me down to Africa
Down to the River Nile
Let me wash away my sorrows
Let me see a brighter tomorrow
Let me always praise up Jah Jah
Africa is calling, calling, calling my name
Africa is calling, calling, calling my name
Take me down to Africa
My original home
Now my soul can set free
Never to ever roam
Africa is calling, calling, calling my name
Africa is calling, calling, calling my name

Africa

Take me to my mother Africa
Take me to my mother Africa
So she can sooth my very soul
Comfort my whole being
Making me whole
Take me to my mother Africa
Take me to my mother Africa
So she can renew me
Hold and mold me
I was lost but now I'm found
In Africa's embrace
In Africa's care
In Africa's love
Take me to my mother Africa
Take me to my mother Africa
Now I'm home

All Lives Matter

Kiss me Ratid, Kiss me Ratid
Police a take us for target
Police a take us for target
Brutality!
Brutality!
Police brutality
Another fatality
On one end the police who should be protecting
should be serving
On the other end laying dead is a Black bother
This is not new, a long time this been going on
still I'm going to shed my little light
on this craziness to Rass to Rass
I'm going to burn a fire on these corrupted and cruel cops
America!
America!
This has to stop
All lives matter
America these are the facts it's always a Black life
that's taken in such cruel fashion
America! America!
What's this, what's that?
What's up with these racists cops?
Fire burn, Fire burn
Fire burn
This has a lot of citizens seeing red
The outcome going to be dread
We need to see this end
We need peace in our city streets
All lives matter
All humans bleed
An eye for an eye

A tooth for a tooth
is not the answer my youths
Government step up, step in put a leash on these beasts
They wear the uniform of brutality
They have a license to kill, they target Black people at will
If man don't stop them, Father surely will
It's a hard pill to swallow when an innocent life is put to chill
One time the cry was: justice for the poor
Now it's a universal cry justice for the dead
Remember citizens
All lives matter!
All lives matter!

All that

Gal a you got all that
Gal you firm and fat
From front to back
Wait is pump you pump up that
A you pad up that
All this fixing as if for tricking
Wait!
Scare them fear them
Me out to scream
Nothing on you is for real
All this fixing all this mixing
Just for tricking
You're going to get a beating
Gal a you got all that
Gal you sexy and fat
From front to back
I need to get some of that
Slip slap where your booty at
A so-so straight back
A how you pull off that
Wait!
A pump you pump up that
A you pad up that
Your skin is clean
Please say it real
And it's not bleach
Screech to a halt stop!
Gal you fake from bottom to top
You need to stop that
Gal a you got all that
Gal you firm and fat
From front to back

A time me take some of that
Wait identify your gender
Please! Please! Make it warm and tender
And of the feminine gender
So for you I can surrender

All Things Jamaican

Kiss me Blue Draws and Drops
Wait a Grater cakes! Give me two of that
Please tell me a no fool my eyes a fool me
You got Toto, you start up my motor
From me a boy me a eat Toto
If I what! If I would! Oh yes I would!
Give me two slices of the Potato Pudding
No bother to hold back, bag up six Grater
Cakes and half a dozen Drops
Wait me nose not deceiving me, is Turn
Cornmeal me smell around a back
Dish out a bowl carry come quick
I'm going to lick these two Veggie Patty for six
Then is when you was going to tell me
You have Flush Top Pone
You just tickle my funny bones
A lie you a tell, is Aunt Daisy make the Gizzada
Child you well out of order
Hold there, stop there mind you make me fart
You couldn't tell me you got Plantain Tarts
I not lying, Jamaican Pastry Delight will satisfy any appetite
Right now my appetite-slack me a eat two slice of Jenny Favorite Cake
If I fall asleep don't shake, I a hold a meditate

Almighty Pum Pum

Almighty Pum Pum
I pray to thee
For you to treat me right
Morning noon and mostly at nights
Almighty Pum Pum
You possess the power to control minds
You make men walk, run for miles
You make men lie, steal, and cheat
You make man take pills, tonic, and all kind of boost up
Almighty Pum Pum
You give birth and begin new life
You also can take a life
You have the ability to take in and push out
You can be loud you can be quiet
You come pon tall, short, slim, big, brown, black, and white bodies
And all is equally as powerful
Almighty Pum Pum
You can be tight you can be loose
Some of your owner keep you natural
Some decorate you up
You look good with tattoos you look good with piercings
Some man have preference some don't care
Men just love you all the same
Almighty Pum Pum
It's not always your fault how you end up
Breed up breed up
Your owners sometimes get careless and leave you up to chance
Most man no ramp with Pum Pum
All man think they can mash up Pum Pum
Pum pum have a way of convincing us men
say we a don – Pum Pum generals
If Pum Pum was a game in the Olympics I would be a gold medalist

———

Pum Pum have nuff powers
Pum Pum start wars
The more I get it is the more I want it
Pum Pum have a magnet that pulls men in
Pum Pum know when you good, Pum Pum know when you bad
Pum Pum kill nuff men
Nuff man kill some good Pum Pum
Old idiots them
Look how much Pum Pum on this Earth
Too much to mention all the different nationality of Pum Pum
Almighty Pum Pum
This I want to declare you're bad
Me convince pum pum got eye
Me done know it got mouth, tongue, lips, and cheeks
I wonder if in secret Pum Pum can speak
Pum Pum can bite even though it don't have any teeth
If you know how to handle Pum Pum
Oh lord it sweet, it sweet, it sweet, it sweet
Almighty Pum Pum you're the best
I put you through nuff test
Now me know it can't done
Your owners just wash it up
And keep you hidden behind plenty style of baggies
Pum Pum a no all style of draws make you look good
When your owner find the right fit
You're a dish you're every man's wish
I could care less if I have to take off draws or draws drop already
Me no care if you stay still or move, me will find my own groove
Some owners brag about their Pum Pum
Some keep it as a secret only their man can reveal it
Almighty Pum Pum
Some owners give it up for free some charge a fee
Me no care me just love Pum Pum plenty
It's not all the time but I will take another man Pum Pum
Me not going to lie and me not saying I wouldn't do it
A nuff man taste Pum Pum

Pum Pum how you can make man get vex so easily?
Then in seconds make us so happy
I learned to accept that Pum Pum rule
A nuff boy want to go to Pum Pum School
It take years of practice to get a Pum Pum degree
Me personally prefer when Pum Pum free
A nuff owners charge me a Pum Pum fee
Me just a get caught up with some of the late fees
Almighty pum pum
I pray to thee
All when I am old please be nice to me
May I be able to sample a few more Pum Pum?
Before I leave

At The End

When you're getting closer to your rainbow
Don't stress it as a so Jah-Jah set it
Your pot of gold was always in your heart
Sing your hallelujahs
Sing your holy, holy
Get ready to receive your glory
You're a star, you've shone you light here on earth
Hopefully you found your true worth
When you're getting closer to light out
No need to shout
Stay calm
All man walk this walk
All humans get the same chance to receive full circle
Sing your hallelujahs
Sing your holy, holy
Get ready to receive your glory
You're a star, you've shone your light here on earth
Hopefully you found your true worth

Back Away

I woke with a wonderful vibes and feelings
So back away with your conniving
Your back door dealings
Don't come so early with your mouth leaking
So-so rumors you're spreading
I start my day on a great rhythm
Don't need your bad energy
A Jah me a praise
Move with your evil ways
I woke with all eyes open
Back away with your side door dealings
Your labba, labba, mouth leaking
Your lies telling
Your science working
Your devil working
Your isms and schisms
The fire that you are burning
Your bad words cursing
Your bad odor spreading
Your virus that you are carrying
The pit that you are digging
Your evil ways of thinking
Back away
Back away
Back away

Black Man Struggle

Black man struggle
Black man juggle
See my Black brother
Searching trash bins looking for pint bottles
Black man struggle
Black man juggle
His heavy bag a jingle
Click, clank a few bottles smash
Black man struggle
Black man juggle
See my Black brother
Day in day out walking the same old route
His strong Black skin dripping with sweat
His big feet was made to carry his frame
Battered bruise and damage
I feel his Pain
He has mile to walk balancing his heavy load on his head
Such a life is dread
Black man struggle
Black man juggle

Black Woman

Jah know me love look upon Black woman
I can't lie
I hope to love them till the day I die
Every Black woman is an Empress, a Queen and a Princess
Regardless of the stress
They must be treated no less
Jah know me love to see Black woman
I can't lie
Sometimes I wonder why, they come in such
wonderful flavors to suit every guy
Black woman has been put through the worst of times
Yet with their heads held high they multiply
They are graced by the love of the Most High
Every Black woman is an Empress, a Queen and a Princess
No matter the race, backgrounds or religious beliefs
They're all a beautiful vision
Black woman know thyself
Respect thyself
Be proud of thyself
You're all unique a one of a kind creation
Beautiful in and out, your beauty can't be compared
Black woman there is no room to share
Know your worth, only then you'll lower the length of your skirts
Respect your talents
Love your ebony soft sexy skins
Your eyes mirror inner heaven
Black woman you're dark and lovely
Perfect in every way
Jah know me can't lie
I can't lie
I love to see Black woman
I love their fashions
I love their styles
I hope to love them till the day I die

Born Free

By: Mia Atre & Vernon Paddy

You born free
Your mother born free
Your daddy born free
Your great great granny born into slavery
Let's not forget
Let's try to forgive
So we can move forward and live
The name of the game is survival
It's not a sing along revival
You born free, you born free
You born come enjoy all liberties
You born free
You mother born free
You daddy born free
Your great great grandfather born into slavery
You born free, you born free
Respect to those who fought against brutal slavery
You born free, you born free
Into a democratic run society
With your freedom of speech
Your man given rights to vote
Your rights without fear to practice a Religion
Freely to educate oneself
You born free, you born free
Respect to those who endured wicked slavery
You born free
Your mother born free
Your daddy born free
Let's never forget the many African
They were brought here by force to start

Living and dying in slavery
They were sold and auctioned off like animals
Families torn apart to live and die on different plantations
They were treated less than crap
Yet momma's tits was good enough to suckle your babies
While hers lay nearby hungry and dirty
Momma's body was good enough to fulfill master's sick desires
In the cover of night momma body was right
When day break you lash her back with the whip
Slavery was sick, sick, sick
You born free, you born free
You born come enjoy all liberties

Build Up

We have to build up, we have to build up
Build up ourselves
Build up others
We have to lend a helping hand across the land
We have to help our little brothers and sisters
To rise from low vibes and reach higher heights

No man is an island
No man stands alone
Each and every man is my brother

We have to build up, we have to build up
Build up ourselves
Build up others
We have to understand each man's plight
Show love and compassion
We have to help our little brothers and sisters
Rise up out of poverty
We have to encourage them to feel Irie

No man is an island
No man stands alone
Each and every man is my brother

We have to build up, we have to build up
Build up ourselves
Build up others
We have to give more to receive less
We have to show love and nothing else
We have to help our little brothers and sisters

Reach and know their true potential
Realizing their worth on Earth

No man is an island
No man stands alone
Each and every man is my brother

Child

Child of love
Child of beauty
My child
God's gift to me
A creation through man and woman
A blessing for all to see

Child of love
Child of beauty
My child to cherish endlessly
A unique mirror in which I see me in history

Child of love
Child of beauty
My child Savanna
One of my gifts from God
A creation through man and woman
A blessing for all to see

Civil Unrest

Civil unrest
Leading up to full scale war
Ukraine set for full destroy
The people they're fed up
The people they can't take it no more
They want the Government to step up
It's time they set it straight
Or
There'll be hell to pay
Citizens marching through the streets
Searching and destroying
Their Babylon system
Old time smash and grab
They're ripping and robbing
Releasing prisoners of political affiliations
Citizens a flee
Citizens making a plea
Security on tight alert
What's the people worth?
Ashes to ashes dust to dust
Ukraine is about to bust
Things look worse
Civil unrest
Leading up to full scale war
Ukraine set for full destroy
Jah see and know
I pray the innocent don't feel most of the blows
I hope the government step up
Set it up
Get things right
Their citizens bringing the fight
Bringing the fight
Bringing the fight

Clean Heart

Live life as a clean heart Rasta
Joy and laughter
With Jah the I will prosper
Live life humble
Your feet won't stumble
Babylon grubs won't let your stomach grumble

Live life as a clean heart Rasta
Peace and love
With Jah the I will prosper
Live life clean
Your mind won't be weak
Babylon system won't lead you astray

Life is filled with lots of barriers
Each will burn in his or her own fire
To fulfill their destiny
Enjoy life journey
Respect the destination
Live and tell your own story
Leave behind your own legacy

Live life as a clean heart Rasta
With clean hands and a pure heart
You and Jah will never part
Jah is the foundation
Be a strong root
Your tree will bear sweet and plenty fruits
Your fellow men will see your examples
Some will follow, some will find their own path of destruction

Shine your own light
Live your own life
Write your own story
Create your own history
Life is a pure and wonderful mystery
Let you be known
Walk good and it will show

Confusion

Total confusion amongst nations
Identity crisis amongst many
Man and man confused
Man want to be woman
Woman want to be man
What a bam bam so many a go get slam
It's so ill it can't be Jah will
Total confusion, total confusion
Man to love oneself
Man must respect oneself
Love to live within your own skin
Stop the bleaching
Stop the hair straightening
Love your Congo-ness
Love your locks
Respect the hair on your head
How are you going to face the Father
When you change how you fava
Man to love the true him
Don't change Jah plan
Plenty live for fame
Mix up in the wrong game
Plenty worship vanity
Hoard up all their money
Kind words replace with profanity
No more love for humanity
Try to tame your tongue, shut your big mouth
It's time to change your route
We're tired to hear your screams and shouts
So many slipping
Jah going to put on the whipping
Total confusion, total confusion

Identity crisis amongst men
Man and man confused
Man a dress in woman clothing
Woman a dress up like man
Plenty idolize man, that's not Jah plan
Change your trip or face Jah whip
Love to live within your own skin
Stop rearrange your face, it's a real disgrace
What you're going to tell your maker
When you change how you fava
You don't love your mother and father?
You don't respect JAH JAH
A total confusion, a total confusion

Corona Thing Pt 2

I can't take this Corona thing Natty!
A one week now I don't see my fatty
This Corona thing set a way
It out fe make Rasta stray
My heart is willing
But I flesh is weak
They say we must stay put
I'm about to go roam street

I can't take this Corona thing Natty!
A one week now I don't see my fatty
Bird can't fly on one wing
It's like I got to get a new song to sing
This Corona thing set a way
It out to make Rasta stray
They say we must sit it out
They say we must hold a flex
This Corona thing got Rasta vex

Corona Thing

I can't take this Corona thing you know Natty
The city on lock down
We good weed is in the country
We smoke up what we had here in town
This Corona thing got I nervous
A six texts alone on my phone from Precious
She can't see I Natty she set away
Natty you done know how them stay
I can't take this Corona thing you know Natty
Money in my pockets
Still I can't get anything a shop to buy
We have to go back to the roots
How Granny did it
Cook food and flour with butter
Fry dumplings throughout the day
Hot water steady a boil
Tea drinking all the time
This Corona thing look like it not going to ramp
A whole lot of people spirit a go cramp
The good suffering for the bad all the time
So Natty! You just sit and silent so
You no got nothing to say
So that's all you a say
You and Corona not going to mingle
You a hold your space
You no got any fear of Corona
For a Jah-Jah you praise
I say that too
Yes Natty fe true

Crappy Shoes

Me and my crappy shoes
Have stories to tell
We've been through hell
Just passing Mandeville
Heading to kill some city
Me and my crappy shoes
The sole is worn out
I feel the heat from the city streets
Burning my feet
Me and my crappy shoes
Got ways to go yet
I have developed this strong mind set
Trying hard to not get upset
I just step in some dog mess
Oh crap, oh crap
A wha this, a wha that
A no dog mess, it's human defecate
Me and my crappy shoes
The miles of abuse
Hills and valleys, narrow tracks and scary alleys
We keep moving no time to skylark
This isn't Miami or New York
A Spanish Town
They don't use Peso or Pound
You better have a nanny
Me and my crappy shoes
Worn, tired, feeling the blues
Wishing I had a new pair of shoes
Tha one ya buss, split and crack
A so-so foot bottom that, calloused harden and tough
It no easy it rough
A man say a few more miles to go

A wa him know
Sun hot even though it a set
Survival on my mind
Need a safe place to rest
The journey isn't done yet
Kill some city I have to get to
U.S. Embassy my final destination
A visa I a try get
This place me a lef
A plane I want to tek
Tired of these mean streets
My crappy shoes and I will have to keep on footing
Keep on walking you think it crap I'm talking
You wouldn't want to walk a mile in my crappy shoes

Craven

Niggy, niggy naggy, naggy
Want te, want te
All the time
It seems needs and wants is all that's on your mind
Settle make it rest
She a bleed at every seams
To fulfill your needs
"Craven choke puppy dog"
Niggy, niggy naggy, naggy
Want te, want te
All the time
It seems needs and wants is all that's on your mind
She a halla she a bawl
To all your wants
Take this now, till later you get the rest
Your hands out stretch a just tek you a tek
You couldn't care less
"Bird who fly too fast fly pass their nest"
Niggy, niggy naggy, naggy
Want te, want te
All the time
It seems needs and wants is all that's on your mind
Have a heart make time pass
Before you reach out and want
You don't hear how her heart is beating fast
Stress and depress
Never the less you still a take
"Puss and dog no have the same luck"

Crime Spree

Your mother making a plea
Your father disagree
They want to try you as an adult
Even though you're only sixteen
You out there in a crime spree
You out there in a crime spree – you out there in a crime spree
You out there in a crime spree
Now you a bawl how you need a break
This is a fact not fiction
You will reap what you sow
Young or old
So live your life clean
For all to see

You mother a cry out to the public a look for our justice
She want our sympathy
She easy forget
You out there in a crime spree – you out there in a crime spree
You out there in a crime spree – you out there in a crime spree
Discipline start in the home
You got to bend the tree before it get old
Set example for other to follow
Get a grip before a child slips
Don't be afraid to put on the whip
We wouldn't get to this
Another child lost
Lost, lost, lost
To Rass, to Rass to Rass
They'll run him through the legal shit-tem
Publicize him as a brute
Forgetting say him a just a young youth
He'll face many barriers in society

A lost child all because of the decisions he made
Should we forgive?
Should we forget?
Should we be his judge, juror and executioner?
Next they might want us to be the heavenly Father

Crossing the River

When I cross the river I am not coming back
When I cross the river I am not coming back
For Jah will be waiting there for me
Jah will be waiting there for me
Waiting there for me
Oh!
Not coming back, not coming back, not coming back
Not coming back, not coming back, not coming back

When I cross the river I am not coming back
When I cross the river I am not coming back
For Jah Jah will hold my hands and lead me to the promise land
The promise land, the promise land, the promise land
Oh!
I am not coming back, not coming back, not coming back
I am not coming back, not coming back, not coming back

When I cross the river I am not coming back
When I cross the river I am not coming back
For with Jah Jah I shall stay, enjoying the rest of my days
In his eternal care
With his forever love, forever love, forever love, forever love
Oh!
I am not coming back, not coming back, not coming back
I am not coming back, not coming back, not coming back
When I cross the river to be with Jah Jah
On that wonderful day, oh on that wonderful day
For Jah will be waiting there for me
Jah will be waiting there for me
Waiting there for me
Oh!
I am not coming back, not coming back, not coming back
I am not coming back, not coming back, not coming back

Dance with Me

Dance with me sweet ballerina
Dance with me
Dance the dance of love
Dance the dance of love
Dance the dance of love
All night

Dance with me sweet ballerina
Dance with me
Dance the dance of love
Dance the dance of love
Dance the dance of love
Dance with me till we're old and gray
Hold my hands to life's every song
Never leave, say you'll stay

Dance with me sweet ballerina
Dance with me
Dance the dance of love
Dance the dance of love
Dance the dance of love
Let's dance to remember, never to forget
Let's dance with no regrets
Let's dance till our dying breath

Dance with me sweet ballerina
Dance with me

Death and Destruction

Death and destruction in the streets
Death and destruction in the streets
None of it is sweet
Modern technology allows us to see it
Cries are heard loud and clear
We only want our equal share
We need things to be fair
We no longer want to live in fear
For years we have been hunted
It's like having daily dreams that is haunting
It's like having a target on your back
From just being born Black
Death and destruction in the streets
Death and destruction in the streets
None of it is sweet
Modern technology allows us to see it
Fires are burning hot
There are crucial spots
Protesting and demonstrating
For years we are waiting
Anticipating these changes
The broken system is fucked
Such is such
They themselves know
They have allowed the innocent death toll to rise
Sitting high on their backsides
They heard the citizen's cries
Now they are burning and looting tonight
They are all ready to fight
Wait! We have done that for years
Just to get some rights
That they abuse day and night
America we have taken two step forward and three steps back
America! They are ready to burn this mother

51

Death

Death is sure
Death is a must
Death is for all of us
Love life
Love self
Death is a passage for all of us
Live life
Enjoy time
Time is given and time is taken
Death is a part of living, it's the end
Respect life
Love your friends
Death don't have to be the end
Death is Christ Jesus
Can be the start of life everlasting
Endless living
Live right
Live for Christ
Trust in him with all your might
There is a reward for you and me
Death is sure
Death is a must
Death is for all of us
Love life
Love your brothers love your sisters
Love husbands love wives
Live clean you'll enter paradise
remember salvation is free
Jesus Christ died for you and me

Defending Jah-Jah

Put on your Gospel armor, put on your Gospel armor
Suit up to defend the Creator
Get ready to fight for Jah-Jah
Good over evil every time, good over evil every time

Put on your Gospel armor, put on your Gospel armor
Suit up to defend the Mighty Father
Righteousness is all we're after, righteousness is all we're after
Equal rights and justice for all

Put on your Gospel armor, put on your Gospel armor
Suit up and feel the power, suit up and feel the power
Have no fear
Jah-Jah will be with you always
as you fight the good fight
Fight with all your might
Peace on Earth for all mankind
Let respect and love flow freely
Clear your mind, clear your mind
Feel the power from the Man on High

Put on your Gospel armor, put on your Gospel armor
With his words you can conquer
No evil can enter, no evil can enter
Suit up to defend the Creator
Get ready to fight for Jah-Jah
You're covered in the new light of the Mighty Father
Your new light is shining brighter
You're ready for any fight
Remember Jah is by your side
You wear the suit of righteousness
Nothing and no one can test
The Gospel armor is the best

Deleting

Spend the day deleting
All the negative
All the old deceiving
All the back biting
All the drama
All the soap opera
All the lies and cheating
Out of my system
Spend the day deleting
Bad vibes
Bad mind
Bad ways
Out of my system
Spend the day deleting
Your text messages
Spend the day deleting
Oh how I feel relived
Such a wonderful feeling
You're no more needed
You have been deleted

Do You, Have You Ever?

Do you ever think of me, even for a few
seconds in your twenty four hours?
Do you ever wish for me all the good and best of a day?
Do you, have you ever?
Do you ever care enough to wonder how I survive?
What are my fears?
How I cope with my daily strife?
Do you, have you ever?
Do you wonder if I pray?
Do you ever think of me, even for a few seconds in your precious day?
When was the last time you mentioned my name?
Wonder how I'm surviving this game?
Do I point fingers, placing the blame?
Why didn't I seek fortune or fame?
Life is a vicious game every human has to play till their lives are up
Don't judge don't think I'm weak or lame
I didn't choose this life
I'm just caught up into this world wind of living within this skin
Within my race
Being a poor human sure feels like a crime
It blows my mind
Morning, noon and at nights
Do you see me from eyes that see color
Or from eyes that see human suffering and strife?
Do your ears hear human cries?
Do you, have you ever
Taken the time to see how the other half is living
Right in your towns and cities?
Do you have any pity?
For those who live so desperate, so lonely in deplorable conditions
While you live cozy and secure
Do you, have you ever?

Don't Forget Me when I'm Gone

Don't forget me when I'm gone
Mention my name on Father's day
Think of me around Christmas time
For all the right reasons
In this the best season
Remember me around spring
With all the beautiful flowers, plants
And all living things
Remind yourself of how I did love summer
The heat, the rain
Having fun with my family
The trips
The drives that got harder as time went by
From the diming of my eye sight
From my enlarge prostate
Don't forget me when I'm gone
Remember my many teachings
The love I poured onto you all
The kindness I gave
The forgiveness was divine
Remember Jah
Never forget he loves you all the best
Hopefully I made a great impression
On you all
That my actions spoke louder than words
Don't forget me when I'm gone
I hope the choices I made
Was in the best interest of you all
My regrets are few
My love is endless for you all
Don't forget me when I'm gone
I'm sorry for any inconveniences

If any goals weren't met in a timely manner
Remember nothing happens before the right time
If there were things you needed
That you didn't get from me
Remember things gained by self is better appreciated
Don't forget me when I'm gone
Know without a shadow of a doubt
I made endless sacrifices for you all
I went without many times
Know my love only grew more with time
Know my pride soared with every achievements
I'm so proud of you all
Love the inner you and respect the outer even more
Find the time to enjoy this short life

Don't Wait

Don't wait for man to leave earth
To know say a Jah come first
Give thanks to the Father
Is him give today and tomorrow
Big up the name of the highest king
Jah
Can't see beyond today
Don't know what tomorrow will bring
I can't see into the future
But to Jah I pray
Giving thanks for another day
Big up the name of the highest king
Jah
Don't wait for man to leave earth
To show some love
To speak some love
Respect Mother Nature
Enjoy Father Time
Is Jah give each seconds
Oh he's the most high
He's the giver of time
Big up the name of the highest king
Jah
Every time

Every Time

Every time I wake up I give thanks to the Almighty
To the Almighty, to the Almighty
When I wake and open my eyes
I give thanks to the Almighty
When I wake and open my mouth
I give thanks to the Almighty
For he give to me, oh how he give to me
My life to live oh it's all his will
All his will, all his will
Oh I give thanks and praises to the Almighty
To the Almighty, to the Almighty
Every time I wake up I give thanks to the Almighty
When I wake and stand on my feet
I give thanks to the Almighty
With a sound mind
I give thanks to the Almighty
For he give to me, oh how he give to me
My life to live, my life to live
Oh it's all his will
All his will, all his will
This love in my heart I'll forever give to him
To Jah only, to Jah only
For he secures me
For he reassures me
Oh how Jah Jah love controls me
Every time I wake up I give thanks to the Almighty
To the Almighty, to the Almighty
When I wake and my kids I see
The love for Jah Jah is all around me
For he give to me, oh how he give to me
My life to live, oh it's all his will
All his will, all his will
Oh I give thanks and praises to the Almighty

Fear

The World is in fear
It's in the news everyday
Fear of flying to get somewhere
As so many planes are being bombed and crashed
They seem to always disappear
Terrorism, sabotage oh Jah
The World is in fear
So much natural disasters
Hurricanes, earthquakes, floods and fires
What a year 1988
A year to remember
So many have died
So many have cried
Oh Jah help me to not worry
To face the harsh realities
We're in a World of fears

Five Parts of a Heart

Five parts of a heart
My heaven on earth
My pride and my joy
Four girls and a boy

Five parts of a heart
My heaven on earth
My whole being
Body soul and mind on fire
Knowing how
I adore you five

Five parts of a heart
My heaven on earth
You all make it right
Morning noon or night

Five parts of a heart
My heaven on earth
You're all equal in worth
You're
Your own uniqueness
All full of greatness

Five parts of a heart
My heaven on earth
Little innocent eyes
Mirroring clear and clean vibes

Five parts of a heart
My heaven on earth
Gently touch oh! How I love you five so much

Five parts of a heart
My heaven on earth
Calm voices, so sweet
Laughter to last my lifetime

Five parts of my heart
My heaven on earth
Hope you all live strong
Long
Enjoying
Heaven on earth
As I have through you five

Fleeting Illusion

By: Mia Atre & Vernon Paddy

You have become a fleeting illusion
When you were my number one
Some say you're playing hard to get
I think it's the dread you forget
Things in new perspective
My heart is checked
This I can't forget
All our give and take
The ups and downs
The many turning around
The hits the misses
I have no regrets
Your love was simply the best
Oh way above the rest
You were the true Empress
You have become a fleeting illusion
A figment of my imagination
A dream from reality
The love bubble burst
Puff up like smoke
Was our love a joke?
Wasted time, how do I forget?
When your love was ever bless
My sweet Empress

Fog of War

When the fog of war is cleared
When the dust is settled from the air
Body count is taken
Rights and wrongs are established
War not funny and it's all about the money
When the families of fallen soldiers get old glory
The dead is given twenty one gun salute
War not funny and it's all about the money
The politricks of war between countries
The get and the give
War not funny and it's all about the money
When the fog of war is cleared
The aftermath of destruction by hands of men
With new technology and modern weapons
Wars are fought with more advice given by bright minds
Men who only study warfare
War not funny and it's all about the money
With greed on men's minds it only brings cruelty
Towards others
Countries have been training men for combat since Jesus Christ was
Brutally crucified on the cross
War not funny and it's all about the money
When the fog of war is cleared
When the dust is settled from the air
When both sides take stack of their infrastructure damages
Estimating cost
To Rass to Rass to Rass to Rass
War not funny and it's all about the money
There is no true winners of any war
Only losers
When was it ever right to take another brothers life
Countries fighting for power

When only Jah Jah know the hour
Jah build this world
Who gave men the right to divide?
To have
Boundaries and Borders
To put restriction on others to move freely from here to there
Is this one world big enough for all of us?
To Rass to Rass to Rass to Rass
War not funny and it's all about the money

For Erick Reynolds

When I get the news I started to cry
I had to sit back
They had to repeat it twice
They told me Lapp drop
Lapp heart stop
I closed my eyes
I started to think back on times
Times at Uncle Fred yard
Me, Lapp, and Kenrick kicking soccer
The many days spend down a ball ground
Clowning around such fun and laughter
Watching you playing Cricket
Rock fishing in-between Uncle Fred and Extabi
Diving off enjoying our sweet paradise Negril
The quiet ways about you
That handsome smile
Your unique laughter
Immediately I start praying to Jah Jah
Oh Mighty and forgiven Father
Hold Lapp into your comfort
Take him with you to be in peace
We will miss the physical
Lapp was very spiritual
Lapp had cleans hands and a pure heart
Lapp and Jah will never part
We will keep Lapp into our hearts
The Spirit lives it never dies
Our tears will always flow
Our emotions will forever show
Sleep well
Son
Brother
Uncle
Father

For My Brother Terrence

Fight the good fight
Fight that good fight
Fight, fight, fight
We're all here standing by your side
Hope you can feel the mighty wave of encouragement,
love and well wishes coming your way
Fight the good fight
Fight that good fight
Fight, fight, fight
Keep fighting my brother

For The Love of Life

For the love of life
For the beauty of sight
For knowing wrong from right
I give thanks to Jah
For the love of life
For the years of living
For my health
For my wealth
For my kids
The many treasures of magical memories
Stored up over time through vibes
Living and taking care of self
Care of family
Care of friends
I give thanks to Jah
For the love of life
For my faith
For my beliefs
For all my sins so easily forgiven
For heaven is for real
Please believe
Jah love all humans
His creation
He holds the master plan
He controls all lands
He holds us in the palm of his hands
His love is endless
His love in internal
I give thanks to Jah
To Jah only

For Uncle Prince

Mighty God and merciful Father King of Kings our Savior
Hold uncle Prince
Hold his hands
Hold his hands lead him to the promise land
Lead him to go meet his mother
Lead him to go meet his father
Lead him to go meet his brother
Lead him to go meet his sister

Mighty God and merciful Father King of Kings our Savior
Hold uncle Prince
Hold his hands
Hold his hands lead him to go take his heavenly rest
This man is amongst the best
Can't value his worth here on earth

Mighty God and merciful Father King of Kings our Savior
Let uncle Prince lay upon your chest
Now he is with you a take his endless rest
Shine your light upon him
His work here is done but just start with you in Heaven
Let him see your majestic face and share in your grace

Mighty God and merciful Father King of Kings our Savior
Hold uncle Prince
Hold his hands
Hold his hands lead him to the promise land

Foreign Mind

The blessings of Jah have come to me, thus have set my soul free
My every thought was of you, how lovely it all felt
Suddenly I realized it was all in my head, I had to cool
Settle my foreign mind
Me no mingle into high class society
What's it to you anyway, so just cool
Still I want to carry on, see how far I could get
Why worry and fret I haven't got nothing yet
Deep into my heart I wonder
How lovely it would be to be loved or be loving you
Foreign mind and local body
Every day you wonder what you going to do to get a foreign
For a taste of the sweet foreign life
Some say it's a land where milk and honey flows
When I reach a foreign is only hard work and blows I know
Lazy minded people will fall along the way
For when you come a foreign
This is something you can't portray, it's a hustle, and it's a bustle
Your boss always on your back
Back! Back! Back!
A back a yard you want go already
Boy you try your uttermost to reach, so just cool
Just settle your foreign mind, for what you a go do back a yard
You no sell your father canoe and leave your
poor mother to live off nothing
Now you come a foreign you see it no easy to live foreign lifestyle
I did get a work on a ship washing plates for two-and-six
Me get a promotion as a bar waiter
Selling drinks like strawberry daiquiri and Pina coladas
Yes sir, yes mam
For $2.50 put a prep in your step, a glide in your stride
Have the booze on your sea cruise

Who tip settle big, who don't well me a fret
For I have wife and children and them no reach pool side yet
Me get an order from the passengers get
the drinks from the bar tenders
Serve my drinks promptly, present my check,
and make my change correctly
Tell them about the Excellency
These are the proper procedures of the Poseidon Company
The food is something next I have to talk about
Every day you work hard hungry bust your shirt
When you go to eat your meal
It's either too salty, too greasy like the proportions of the bloody Mary
Chefs do better as we don't want to die from hunger any longer
I could go on and on forever
It will only profit me my passport and a one way ticket home
to sunny Jamaica to go hustle and bustle
To go reach a foreign for a taste of the sweet foreign life

Free Up Free Up

Free up
Free up
Free up your mind
My beautiful African sister
Free up
Free up
Free up your mind
My beautiful child
Don't let evil cloud up your thoughts
Don't let hate enter your heart

Free up
Free up
Free up your mind
My beautiful African sister
Free up
Free up
Free up your mind
My beautiful child
Peace and love is all you should talk
Walk your walk let Jah be that path

Free up
Free up
Free up your mind
My beautiful African sister
Free up
Free up
Free up your mind
My beautiful child
Let Jah light shine through thee
Respect the power of the Trinity

Funny How It's You

By: Mia Atre & Vernon Paddy

Funny how it's you
That captivates my very soul
Funny how it's you
That makes me feel these emotions
Fire and ice, love and hate
Funny how it's you
That holds my attention
Funny how it's you
That makes me smile
That makes me cry
Funny how it's you
That came back anew
Firing up the old love between you and I
New sparks from old flames
New vibes to share
Oh how I care
Now you're close
Oh so dear
for you I care
It comes with new fears
You can say we've been there
We've done that
Yet our love stayed intact
Even with the time and space
That separates us
Same time and space brought us back
Oh that's a fact
Funny how it's you
That holds me each day
Funny how it's you

That reassures me
Funny how it's you
That secures me
It's a real peace of mind
Knowing you're mine
Funny how it's you
Funny how it's you
That's my one true love

Gal You a Warrior

Gal you a warrior, Gal you a warrior
Stand firm and look good ya
I'm going to show you how me talawah
As a true born Jamaican
I'm a true and righteous Rasta
No bugga yagga, no jester
Pure love
No hate I festa
Come let me take you to beautiful Manchester
When I'm done with you
You won't want to leave ya
That I guarantee ya
Sweet daughter
I like your walk
I like your talk
Let's not waste time and skylark
Tonight for me you're the only one
Let's hold hands
Let's embrace
Becoming one together
I know you feel the same vibes
I know you know it's right
Let's make tonight, the night
Sweet sweet daughter
You got the Rasta heart a beat ya
Oh how I love your touch
This love sweet ya
You're now a part of the Rasta
I will make you an Empress
Show you love and pure respect
In every and all aspect
Sweet sweet daughter

Generation

Father G, Father G, Father G
Father G, Father G, Father G
Oh how I often sit and think of thee
All the wonderful life stories you told me
When I was just a little boy pickney
Your memories will live on
I love my generation them, I love my generation them
I love them from the start straight to the end
This poem a big up some of them
Aunt C, Aunt C, Aunt C
Aunt C, Aunt C, Aunt C
Fond memories time spent a your beautiful yard
You always give me a treat
Always something sweet
Plus your sweet jelly coconut water
They help me to make my two daughters
I love my generation them, I love my generation them
I love them from the start straight to the end
This poem a big up some of them
Uncle Claud and Aunt Gloria, Uncle Claud and Aunt Gloria
Uncle Claud and Aunt Gloria, Uncle Claud and Aunt Gloria
What a couple of gems
The amount of fun time down a your yard
With Richie, GG, Yvonne, June, PJohn, and Ivor them
The late evening fish dinners
Living by the sun, stars and moon
Your yard was crowded but we had lots of space
Heaven is graced with both your beautiful face
I love my generation them, I love my generation them
I love them from the start straight to the end
This poem a big up some of them
Aunt Edith, Aunt Edith, Aunt Edith

Aunt Edith, Aunt Edith, Aunt Edith
Words can't express of how you were heavenly sent
A giver to the end
A mother to us all, a mother to us all
Big up, love up and sleep well
Your time here on earth well lived
I love my generation them, I love my generation them
I love them from the start straight to the end
This poem a big up some of the
Grand Ma Vie, Grand Ma Vie, Grand Ma Vie
Grand Ma Vie, Grand Ma Vie, Grand Ma Vie
Me use to look into your beautiful eyes
You were tall and slender
I remember, I remember
Words can't express or tell the truth
Oh how me love you
The short time spent with you
Leaves the biggest impact and that's a fact
Grand Ma Vie me use to put on your blue frock
Entertain the guest a Falcon
Some laugh till their belly bottom drop
I love my generation them, I love my generation them
I love them from the start straight to the end
This poem a big up some of them
Grand Pa Fred, Grand Pa Fred
Grand Pa Fred, Grand Pa Fred
Thank you me brethren
I come from a very handsome generation
Grand Pa Fred you were a lady killer
You and your scooter bike
That I like, that I like
You had such style
Just when we a get tight and closer
Father call you home
When I look into the mirror
It's like me a see you in my reflection

Sleep well, sleep well
Grand Pa Fred
I love my generation them, I love my generation them
I love them from the start straight to the end
This poem a big up some of them
Uncle Prince, Uncle Prince, Uncle Prince
Uncle Prince Uncle Prince, Uncle Prince
How could I ever thank you my brethren
When you walk into a room time felt like it stop
You were clean to the bone
There is no denying that
Quiet and sweet
I adore you from head to feet
Those fishing days as a boy use to sweet, sweet, sweet
When Aunt Maud catch me with Rita
You came all the way from Florida
Me worry and fret
Thinking you were going to bust me chest
Only to hear you say
"Boy why you never lock the door"
"I hope you live long and get nuff Pum-Pum galore"
That day seal and sign my love more
Uncle Prince again it's you I adore
Sleep well, sleep well
Uncle Prince

I love my generation them, I love my generation them
I love them from the start straight to the end
This poem a big up some of them
Uncle Linval, Uncle Linval
Uncle Linval, Uncle Linval
Your time cut short me brethren
I can truly say you live it up
Life in the fast lane
As a boy I remember the big motor bikes
Your handsome face and killer smile

The time spent in summers enjoying lazy laid back Negril
In your spacious A frame house
Watching you and the Lynch brothers diving off the rocks
Reggae music down at Yatch Club
Running around Miss Gretel and Papa Will yard
Cows, goats, dogs, cats, and chickens
They had it all
Priceless time for a city boy
Rest well, rest well
Uncle Linval
I love my generation them, I love my generation them
I love them from the start straight to the end
This poem a big up some of them
Sister Yvonne, Sister Yvonne
Sister Yvonne, Sister Yvonne
Day and night I cry of how I miss thee
Where do I begin?
The memories are so much to share
I'll just say of how I miss you my dear
Thanks for the love we shared
You were the belle of the ball
The beauty of them all
You live rich and free
You never afraid to party and spree
Fun and laughter was all you were after
The giver in you gave to the end
The gift you gave to me and my kids priceless
I love you endless
Sleep well, sleep well
Sister Yvonne
I love my generation them, I love my generation them
I love them from the start straight to the end
This poem a big up some of them
Mr. T, Mr. T, Mr. T
My Daddy, My Daddy, My Daddy
Oh Jah you were so merciful and kind to us

You never let our Daddy suffer much
Holy, Holy, Holy
Oh Jah you took him to glory
Daddy your work here is done
Rest in peace perfect peace
I will treasure our history
Time spent together our story
Countless life lessons you show we
You work from sunup to sundown
Oh how you loved when we were always around
Thanks for all the sacrifices you made
For all the love you shared
Sleep well Daddy, sleep well
I love my generation them, I love my generation them
I love them from the start straight to the end
This poem a big up some of them
Chancy, Chancy, Chancy
My sweet Nephew, My sweet Nephew
Jah give you a quarter out of the whole
Don't mean we loved you less
Jah know we love you endless
Your handsome face and captivating grin
Your tight embrace
Your childlike spirit
Not an hour not a day since
I declare and I made that promise
To honor you in words
To keep your memories alive
My love for you will live till the day I die
Sleep well, sleep well, sleep well
Chancy
I love my generation them, I love my generation them
I love them from the start straight to the end
This poem a big up some of them
In loving memories of these beautiful souls
Ida Stone, John Stone, Josiah Stone, Anny Stone, Millicent Stone

Melia Johnson
Winnifred MaWinny Brown
Jenny Myrie, Denzel Myrie & Mapaul, Jolly Myrie, Solomon Myrie
Willington Hylton & Miss Gretel
Bob Lynch, Christopher Lynch, Mark Lynch, Noel Lynch
Lynette Nunes, Kenan Nunes, Marie Denise
Nunes, Angella Nunes Ford
Marie Donaldson, Maggie Donaldson
Billie Reynolds, Eric Lapp Reynolds, Eddie Reynolds
Liza Connell, Uncle C Connell, Uncle Dandy Connell

Get Up and Stand Up

We a go get up and stand up
Stand up for our rights
Every time we turn on the news or read the papers
It's just Saddam or Bin Laden names
We're fed up
We're tired
We can't stand to hear those names
We a go get up and stand up
Stand up for our rights
All the fuss
All the fighting
This crazy Rass war
Who to take the blame
The big house dirty
The big house corrupt
The whole of them a go get pluck
Hang by the neck like a duck
Everywhere you walk
You hear people a talk
Kuwait this, Kuwait that
Who really give a crap?
Iraqi this, Iraqi that
They all have to stop
We a go get up and stand up
Stand up for our rights
We can't avoid a war
The peace talks only calm an already raging storm
To Rass, to Rass, to Rass
To Bumbo klaat

We a go get up and stand up
Stand up for our rights
We're no longer going to live in fear
We're no longer going to bear that name
We're no longer going to play your games
We a go get up and stand up
Stand up for our rights
You hear

Getting Away

You trying to break my spirit but my mind is too strong
You trying to break my spirit but my mind is too strong
You trying to break my spirit but I'm holding on
Your lies can't hurt me anymore
Your verbal abuse is a waste of your time
My head is held high I'm doing fine
I'm heading towards the light
away from your darkness
I'm getting as far away from your evil and madness
You just can't hurt me anymore

You're trying to break my spirit but my mind is too strong
You're trying to break my spirit but my mind is too strong
You're trying to break my spirit but I'm holding on
Your blows can't hurt me anymore
Your deception and tricks are a waste of your time
My heart is getting stronger I'm doing fine
I'm heading towards peace and harmony
away from your gloom and sadness
I'm getting as far away from your evil and madness
You just can't hurt me anymore
I won't let you hurt me anymore

Give

You must love to give to the needy
You too Rass greedy, greedy, greedy
You have Nuff, some don't have any
You have a lot I don't have a penny
You laugh I know you are a two face
Behind my back you're my enemy
Behind my back you're my enemy
Don't store up earthly treasure
Seek first the kingdom of God and all things will be added unto you
Live wise don't live like a fool
You must love to give to the needy
You too Rass greedy, greedy, greedy
Never just live for you think of others too
Don't turn a blind eye to the suffering of others
Have a heart be a part and not apart
Remember Jesus died on the cross
Be a good steward of your finances
Give to the less fortunate
Get a blessing from the Father up above
You must love to give to the needy
You too Rass greedy, greedy, greedy
You have in excess, while another man is stress
Depress at the end of his rope
You sit up high, they sit down low
Jah sees and knows
This is serious don't strike a pose, smirking like this is a joke
You live high on the hog enjoying steaks and roast pork
Your brother on the street can't even inhale your smoke
Scrounging in garbage cans to get their fill
They would enjoy what you just spill
Chill brother man, chill brother man
This can't be the Father's will
You must love to give to the needy
You too Rass greedy, greedy, greedy

Grand Finale

Today I soared through the clouds
Going to a grand finally
Grand finale, grand finale

Today I soared through the clouds
Going to Uncle Prince grand finale
Grand finale, grand finale

Today Uncle Prince was sent off to glory
Holy, Holy, Holy
You're now with Jah in all his glory
Your time on earth well spent
Your history, your story
Your generation will always tell
The many lives you touched in a positive way
You are gone but your story will live with us here
You are gone but your spirit will always be here

Today I soared through the clouds
Going to a grand finale
Grand finale, grand finale

Today I soared through the clouds
Going to Uncle Prince grand finale
Grand finale, grand finale

Greed

You ever wonder if man could control the weather
What seasons he would prefer
Would he use it for a financial gain?
We done know the minds of men and the games they play
You ever wonder if man could control the time
Would he rewind sometime
Would he go back in time?
Would he charge you and I every nickel and dime for the use of time
You ever wonder if man could control life and death
Would he have loads of regrets?
The burden and stress he would bear
People begging for their love ones to come forward again
You ever wonder why man is just a man
The Mighty Creator give us all knowledge and wisdom
So we could understand our limitations
Live clean brothers and sisters
Live up full and right
Wake up and open your eyes

Happy Birthday Mia Sweet Sixteen

It still feels like yesterday
I had to help you get dressed
Had to help comb your hair
Had to strap you into your booster chair
It was your first day of kindergarten
It feels like yesterday
You blurted out spelling the words "Salt" and "Pepper"
While we sat in the car enjoying Wendy's
You were my cheap date for a whole year
It still feels like yesterday
When we walked out the halls of your school
Hands in hands as you skipped along
You said the words exit
Reading the sign above the door
It feels like yesterday
All the missing teeth
You going off to Elementary, Middle, now in High School
It feels like yesterday
When you would come to be by my side
The hugs, the kisses
The laughter, the cries
It still feels like yesterday
There might be a reason why
Even though you're growing up
My eyes see you as that child of all the yesterdays
Today celebrating your sixteenth birthday
Happy birthday Mia
I love you

Hear Me Oh Lord

Hear me, hear me
I'm on bending knees
Looking up to the sky
Hear me, hear me
Oh Lord in prayers
Earth a run dread, earth a run dread
Earth filled with crisis
Why can't men fix it?
Is this your desire oh Lord?
Earth cleansing
Earth quakes, storms, hurricanes, and fires
So much natural disasters
One after the other
Warfare, nuclear, pollution in the atmosphere
People suffering from new allergies each day
Oh Lord hear me as I pray
Oh Lord hear me as I pray
I'm offering up praises to you oh Lord
I'm pleading to you oh Lord
Bless us, guide us, direct us and protect us
Evil is every where
In our thoughts in our actions
I know there will be a reaction
Oh Lord you see how mankind is living
You see all the senseless killings
Is this a part of your big plan
For Earth to cleanse itself
Man to wipe out man
Wars
Rumors of wars
Men seeking power
Men seeking glory

Men seeking honor
Oh Lord hear my prayers
Oh Lord hear my prayers
A full time mankind wise up
Treat each other with kindness
A full time mankind seek you
Seek forgiveness
Accept you as their Lord and Savior
As revelation reveal it
Without you Lord
Man and man a go feel it
Oh Lord hear me as I pray
Oh Lord hear me as I pray

Here Come Poverty Again

Here come poverty again my friend
Here come poverty again
Here come poverty again my friend
Here come poverty again
Poverty not going to stop till it draw my tongue
It was last year I delete poverty
Said goodbye to suffering his brother
Burned a fire on distraction his sister
Then why him a bring his cousins stress and confusion
Is bad words poverty want me to cuss
Watch him! Watch him!
A come with him shameless self
To come take set like dirty body odor
To come irritate me
A cross poverty want to get me cross to Rass in here
Fire! Fire! Fire!
Fire! Burn poverty, Fire! Burn poverty
Here come poverty again my friend
Here come poverty again
Here come poverty again my friend
Here come poverty again
Yow! Yow! You see before me rid myself of poverty
It suck me bone dry, nearly mad me off
I lost everything even my dignity and pride
A Jah and prayers bring me forward
Poverty bright no bulb
To come show his face again
Me and it
If it bad me is an old bitch
I shall lash poverty with my whip
Watch him! Watch him
Old vampire, old blood sucker

Poverty full a smooth talk
It will pack up your head with madness
Poverty will lead you into pure fantasy
Waste your time, mess up your mind
Poverty will take you off you're A game
Turn you into a looser
Poverty is the biggest abuser
Poverty will always let you find Jesus Christ
That is why I know poverty is the Devil in disguise
Here come poverty again my friend
Here come poverty again
Here come poverty again my friend
Here come poverty again
Poverty won't even ease up
Him just a squeeze up, squeeze up
Brush up, brush up
Touch up, touch up
Poverty think me and it a go wrap up again
Me learn my lessons my friends
Once bitten twice shy
Plus poverty too Rass lie
I kill you once
This time me not going to be responsible for my action
Nor the words from my mouth
Last time you got me a walk and shout
Sweet Jesus, sweet Jesus, sweet Jesus
Poverty you're an old snatch and grabber
Craven should've been your name
You got no shame
You're wild, but I got what to tame you
In Jah-Jah name, in Jah-Jah name
Me and you not going to play any more games
As far as I'm concern poverty you're dead
Dead! Dead! Dead! Dead!
Poverty you're dead! Poverty you're dead!

Stop! Trying to get into my head
Trying to mess up my mind
Trying to waste any more of my precious time
Here come poverty again my friend
Here come poverty again
Here come poverty again my friend
Here come poverty again
Poverty you don't hear my new songs
'I'm moving on up'
'I'm stepping out of Babylon'
'Still I rise'
Poverty I beg you stay behind
Plus you don't play fair
You got no love, you show no care
You just love to tear apart
Shattering hopes and dreams
You get off on cries and screams
You love when others suffer
Poverty you're cruel, wicked and dreadful
Poverty you surely is a crime
Government, world leaders
Citizens are pleading, citizens are pleading
We need help to get rid of old Rass poverty
We need help to leave out of slums and ghettos
We want to reach sky high
We want to live poverty free
So we can pay our rent
Put our pots on fire, eat to our desire
Educate our children
Government you got the power
We the poor gave our votes
Try a new thing
Stop killing innocent citizens
Start killing poverty instead
Government help us to kill poverty no
Government help us to rid poverty from society

Poverty is the root to all evil
Poverty leads to crime and violence
It's evident a hungry man is an angry man
Government how long we the citizens have to live into poverty
Government how long we the citizens are going to suffer

History Lean

By: Mia Atre & Vernon Paddy

History lean it bend History isn't your friend
History lean it no straight
History bend trust me it's not your friend
Fine your own story
Trust and believe in your own story
Leave alone his story, her story, and their story
It set to suit them
Trust me it's not your friend
History lean it's not straight
History bend from start to end
They only put into History what they want us to know
The truth the facts you have to search for that
Fine your own story
Trust and believe in your own story
Leave alone his story, her story and their story
It set to suit them
Trust me it's not your friend

I Hope

I hope you never have to feel half the pain
I hope you never have to feel this way
I pray the tables never turn

This ache can't keep inside
Can't hide
Can't camouflage
You got to let it show
Trust me tears got to flow

I hope you never have to feel half the pain
I hope you never have to feel this way
I pray the tables never turn

A heart wasn't made to take such stress
Too heavy a burden to bear
It's a new type of fear
Show me a sign that you care

I hope you never have to feel half the pain
I hope you never have to feel this way
I pray the tables never turn

I only wish you did care
Wanting to be right here
To hold me
Help me through my fears
My pain it's too much for me to bear
Show me a sign that you care

I hope you never have to feel half the pain
I hope you never have to feel this way
I pray the tables never turn

I Was Born Free

I was born free
To enjoy earth
A descendant of great Africans
But
How can we forget history?
Forget slavery
Forget my great forefathers
Who toiled this soil
Build up this great land
Suffered
Cried
Died
So we can have equal rights
Justice
Respect
Pride in oneself

Time is precious life is short
If you have today give thanks
If you get tomorrow praise Jah

I was born free
Born to love
Born in peace
Privilege to receive an education
Enjoy society
Work and to achieve any and all in life
Enjoying my share
Without greed
But
How do we forget our elders?
They fought for our peace

Our equal rights
So we can have justice
So we can enjoy this great land
Fought for what we hold so precious
Freedom, freedom
Freedom
How do we forget history?
Forget slavery
Forget Africa
Our mother land
Who we were, how we lived?
Questions with such little answers
Well we were
Kings, Queens, inventors, farmers, herders, fishermen
Carpenters, builders,
Sailors, great navigators
We enjoyed and practice our own religions, beliefs, cultures, languages
We are from the foundation of everything great
Music, sports, academics, medicine

Time is precious life is short
If you have today give thanks
If you get tomorrow praise Jah
I was born free
To enjoy Mother Nature and some of father time
For as surely as I live one day I shall die
While I am here I know I should live clean
Let my works be seen
Respect earth, respect my fellow man
Respect all woman
Respect my wife
Love and support my family
I have so many great men and woman
Of color

To fashion from
To look up to
To be like wise and not otherwise

Time is precious life is short
If you have today give thanks
If you get tomorrow praise Jah

If I knew

If I knew then what I know now
The many sides of life, the ups and the downs
The trials and tribulations, the cross I would bear
The countless aches and pain, the rivers of
tears, the inner fears, the betrayals
The families and good friends who have
gone on, without much warning
Not giving me the chance to say and do, the things I wanted to
The hurt I have cause so many, the lies I have told
The hearts I have broken, the hellos and goodbyes
The sleepless nights
If I knew then what I know now
The changes in time, the wars, the many rumors of wars
Leaders rising and falling, the revolution
Earth pollution, great greed and corruption
Murder and violence, modern day slavery, poverty and desolation
Homelessness, oh! What a fucking mess
No one seems to really give a crap, oh! That's a fact
Politics or should I say pure tricks
Greed and deception, pocket lining, bank book stuffing
The rich raping the poor, religion water wash,
weak, and the truth have a leak
Books written to suit a certain society
People placed in class, how the hell they can do this to Rass
Most of History shitty
Know your own story, respect oneself
As most don't give a crap about the truth and the facts
Hollywood white wash, pure fantasy, moral
indecency, decay, rotten and spoil
A just bling a the new thing, take time to just listen
To most of these new songs, they aren't teaching anything
The beat sweet, contents weak

We not finger pointing, who the cap fit let them wear it
Chronixx says 'it no take nothing, to go down a Rome and start a fire'
If I knew then what I know now
I would have teach, I would have preached
Like the great Marcus Garvey, to uplift, to enlighten, to love one selves
Bob Marley and Peter Tosh, said it, one love
one heart, equal rights and justice
Heads of Government keep your Rass Peace
Start to clean up our streets, we need better wages
More attention to youth development
More care for the elders, more Justice for the unjust
We Jamaicans easily forget, 'out of many one people'
Society still place, light, bright skin over dark and lovely
A full time that stop, it only causes pain and misery
It's the main cause why them a bleach
Society open up your eyes, let's tell the truth stop all lies
It will easy up the tribal wars, bring back peace in our streets
Let's teach unity, togetherness, and oneness
Let's teach Rasta, peace and love, let's praise Jah

For All The Broken Souls

may you all find your inner warrior
For all the broken minds
may you all re-educate
seek and find the true light

In loving memory of these beautiful souls
Mila Johnson
Violet Arthur
Liza Connell
Millicent Stone
Jenny Myrie
Ida Stone-Lynch
Celeste Stone-Reynolds
Edith Maud Guthrie
Denise Annmarie Nunes
Angella Nunes-Ford
Yvonne C. Browne-Mignott
Aunty Maggy, Aunt Marie Donaldson, Ma Winny Brown
Noel L lynch
Bryan Glaze
Sleep well my people

In Vision

In vision I saw Holy Mount Zion
Majestic bright lights
In vision I heard Jah glorious voice ever clear
Calling, calling, calling I home
Calling, calling, calling I home
I know Zion is where I belong
Oh Zion is where I belong, Oh Zion is where I belong
May I be lucky to behold Jah beauty, to feel Jah Embrace?
Man must live upright
Stop all the fussing, Stop all the fighting
Man must lend a helping hand
As we cross the hills, the gullies and the valleys
The trials and burdens we bear
They never seems fair
Oh JAH is always near
Yet we must all trod this land
Leading to Holy Mount Zion
In vision I heard JAH mighty voice ever so clear
Calling, calling, calling I home, Calling, calling, calling I home
Holy mount Zion is where I belong, Holy mount Zion is where I belong
Oh holy mount Zion, Oh holy mount Zion
Calling, calling I home
In vision I saw Holy Mount Zion
Mystic bright lights
In vision I heard Jah glorious voice ever clear
Calling, calling, calling I home
Calling, calling, calling I home
I know Zion is where I belong
Oh Zion is where I belong, Oh Zion is where I belong
May I be lucky to behold Jah beauty, feel his embrace?
Man must live upright
Get his soul right

Salvation is free, JAH pay the price for we
Don't put JAH on a lay away plan
You'll get leave behind
The time is now not later
Worship Jah in your youth with strength and vigor
So you will enter Holy Mount Zion
When Zion's gates get open I want to be on the inside
I want to bow down give praises to the Almighty
On my knees praying earnestly, oh Jah
protect me, guide and direct me
In Holy Mount Zion
Singing
Oh I'm home, Oh I'm home, Oh I'm home
Holy Mount Zion I'm home

IRMA

Take away yourself Irma
Take away yourself
You're not welcome here Irma
Take away yourself Irma
Take away yourself
We can't accommodate you Irma
You blind deaf and dumb Irma
You don't see we're financially embarrass
We're spiritual stress
We're prayed out
All last week we prayed for Texas
Irma you don't see fires out west
Texas still damp from Harvey's mess
We need a rest
Take away yourself Irma
Take away yourself
You're not welcome here Irma
Take away yourself Irma
Take away yourself
We can't accommodate you Irma
Please don't puff up your chest
A see you out to get vex
I heard you're the biggest
Super bad
Tougher
Stronger than the rest
Please don't roll your big eyes Irma
I beg you don't start to cry
We can't handle your type of heavy rain showers
Irma please don't flap your huge wings
Your powerful might winds
Out to turn everything outside in and inside out

Take away yourself Irma
Take away yourself
You're not welcome Irma
Take away yourself Irma
We can't accommodate you Irma

Jah Me Fear

A Jah me fear, a Jah me fear
No guy can come near
So devil get out of here, so devil get out of here
A beg you hear
Beware
Good over evil
Don't try test, Jah is the best
A Jah me fear, a Jah me fear
A pure love into my heart
No dark thoughts, no dark thoughts
My Father and I will never part
I shall praise up his name for the rest of my days
A Jah me fear, a Jah me fear
No guy can come near
If you're evil doer you can't stay
You got to get out of here, you got to get out of here
A beg you hear
Beware
Good conquers evil every time
Don't try test
Jah is the very best
A Jah me fear
A Jah me fear
A Jah me fear

Jah Run Things

Oh yes Jah is the mighty king of all kings
A Jah run things, a he run things
Old Devil worshippers get on your knees
Start to think
Surrender! Surrender!
You know you can't win
Oh yes Jah is the mighty king of all kings
A Jah run things, a he run things
Put Jah into your heart
You and he will never part
Put Jah in everything
Call on his name, Jah!
Never be ashamed praise up his holy name, Jah!
Oh yes Jah is the mighty king of all kings
A Jah run things, a he run things
We country need a spiritual wash
To stop all the violence and crap
This is a plea! This is a plea!
Love your brother man, love your family
Lend a helping hand to the weak
Salvation is for all of us
A blessing you shall get, never you forget
So stop from fretting, there is hope for our country yet
Oh yes Jah is the mighty king of all kings
A Jah run things, a he run things
We have to come together as one
How easy we forget
"Out of many we are one"
Let's unite and stay strong
To fight down old Devil workers and Babylon system
Let's preach and teach the Bible
A chapter a day keep the devil away

With Jah on your side
The wicked have to hide
Let's march up and down our streets demanding peace
Peace, peace, peace
More love in our hearts
Prosperity for all
Oh yes Jah is the mighty king of all kings
A Jah run things
A he run things
A he run things

Jah Why?

A no little cry me cry oh Jah why
Why, why oh why Jah
Why, why oh why Jah
You care so much about the I
Oh mighty Jah
You guide I
You protect I
You direct I
Oh mighty Jah
You bless I
Another year I see
I shout praises to Jah All Mighty
A no little cry me cry oh Jah why
Why, why oh why Jah
Why, why oh why Jah
You care so much about the I
I will live my days praising your mighty name
Oh Jah

Journey

Jah go with me
As I start this new journey
This new part of my life
Jah bless me
Jah comfort me
Jah guide me
Jah go with me
As I leave behind the old
To take on the new
Jah bless me
Jah comfort me
Jah guide me
Jah direct me
Jah go with me
Give me peace of mind
Give me clear thoughts
Give me the extra strength
To manage the task at hand
Humble me
Let me give thanks onto thee
Let my prayers never stop
Jah bless me
Jah comfort me
Jah guide me
Jah direct me
Jah go with me
Be there at the end
May my soul find perfect peace
May my deeds please thee, oh Jah

King James

Cleveland on fire
Cleveland on fire
Cleveland on fire
Cleveland on fire
The Cavaliers hot, hot, hot
The Cavaliers hot, hot, hot
King James fulfilled his promise to the people
Proved to the World his greatness
You can't deny the facts
The Cavaliers on top, top, top

Cleveland on fire
Cleveland on fire
Cleveland on fire
Cleveland on fire
The Cavaliers hot, hot, hot
The Cavaliers hot, hot, hot
King James dug out from the bottom
Him and his teammates persevered and reached the top
Prophecy fulfilled
King James brought a championship to Cleveland
The people's hearts jubilant
Celebration time, celebration time
The prodigal son came home
Was forgiven
Now he gave back big time

Cleveland on fire
Cleveland on fire
Cleveland on fire
Cleveland on fire
The Cavaliers hot, hot, hot

The Cavaliers hot, hot, hot
You can't count out a warrior
King James heart is like a lion
What looked like impossible
He made possible
With all the hype
With all the drama
Nothing more can be said
The man just great
Oh yes him and his teammates
Cavaliers hot, hot, hot
Cavaliers hot, hot, hot
Cavaliers reach the top, top, top

Lady

Lady with the red head wrap
This is true
This is a fact
You walk in the room
The light got brighter
Time felt like it stopped
Lady you're hot, lady you're hot

Lady with the red head wrap
White top blue jeans
Lady it screams beauty
Lady you're hot, lady you're hot

Lady you wear the head wrap
You move and time stops
All eyes are on you
Lady with the red head wrap
Lady you're hot, lady you're hot

Lend a Helping Hand

Lend a hand to the elders, lend a hand to the elders
They set the examples for us to follow
Lend a hand to the elders, lend a hand to the elders
Them a the old trend setters
Them a we fathers, fathers, fathers
Lend a hand to the elders, lend a hand to the elders
They set the examples for us to follow
Lend a hand to the elders, lend a hand to the elders
Them a we mothers, mothers, mothers

Show respect to the elders, show respect to the elders
They pave the way for us all
Without them we wouldn't be here
Honor we elders, honor we elders
For all their hard work
For their strength and perseverance
Allow them to live without fear
Take care of our elders, take care of our elders
Help them enjoy their golden days
Show them how we care by holding them close and dear
You hear, you hear
The elders are our fathers
The elders are our mothers

Lies

POEM BY VERNON PADDY & MIA ATRE

Imagine those type of guys
Come on ya and tell Black people pure lies
Want us to believe Father into the sky
Lies, lies, lies
Lies, lies, lies
How we must worship and die to receive
Our reward in heaven up into the sky
Lies, lies, lies
Lies, lies, lies
Your reward is enjoyed right here on earth
From knowing one's worth
The goodness of your heart
Certain type of guy with big bag of lies
Want to brain wash you and me.
Tell we this
Tell we that
How horse dead and cow fat
Pure lies no facts
They want us to drink their wine of violence
Want us to sit back and believe their crap
Lies, lies, lies
Lies, lies, lies
It's time we re-educate and change our mind set
or get leave behind in their false crap
You owe it to yourself to know your story
to truly enjoy your destiny
or die living in fantasy

Life Aboard Ship

This is reality I worked on a ship
Food and sleep day I miss
Rumors spreading your name heading on heroes list
Death you not missing
Every day all you hear is work, work and work
You could be House Keeper or Purser Clerk
Pot Washer or Clock Watcher
Front line or behind
You on the boss man time
I'm having dreams of home
Yes sweet dreams of home
But to go do what?
Hurricane Killbert, drugs along with political crisis
Have the country a way
Me a suffer here and a go suffer there
Plus I will have to live in fear as economic crisis
War and crime a blow poor people minds
On board ship passengers come a sum up things
Thinking things look like fun
Feel say whole heap of money a run
As a bar waiter on the front line
Me not boasting, I'm not toasting
and it's not what I'm smoking
Some let off, and some won't
Then we have a ship load of Baptist
be realistic I'm Christ-like but without money
things look funny, me have rent to pay
Suzie and Evy want them money in a hurry without delay
My kids need to go to school
Don't want them growing up being a fool
My love life boring, my social life gone to the dogs
It's been a long time since I've been laid

I laugh ha, ha, ha it funny things and time tough
There are eyes always watching you, a watch me
A watch you, still if I could get a little honey
I would a spend some of my money
and have some fun without fear
At twenty-eight things getting late
No church bells ringing, no ring giving
It's not funny, it's life aboard ship
There are lots you will always miss
Keep on doing what you're doing, if you know what you're doing
If not, make that change
Sisters you got that power to make that change
Brothers you got the power to make that move

My little friend

I have a little friend named Symone
All day long she live on her cell phone
All day long she's on Facebook
Just a look, just a look
A talk about how she need a man
So
Me introduce her to my friend Mickey
I should tell her how him love to fight
Mickey will fight over everything and anything
All when he can't win
Last week him stab her over fry dumpling
Box her in the face over pumpkin
Beat, beat her up over man thing
Symone invite me over a tell me about the drama
How she can't live no more under such conditions
Mickey no stop beat me into submission
How her life feel like she in a soap opera
How the one Mickey a dictator
How him rule with iron fist
How she can't take no more Rass licks
How she never sign up for none of this
Mickey take her for beaten stick
How her life fill with pure fear
Blood sweat and tears
How she nice body full a batter bruises everywhere
Me tell Symone how me sorry to hear
And how me care
And to hush life no fair
And how the two of them make a great pair
And how she must try to get along me dear
And
That's when I take my time walk away clear
A feel sorry for her you hear

Little Rock

Jamaica the little piece of Africa
The black diamond in the Caribbean
Land of those who endured slavery

Jamaica the little piece of Africa
The black pearl in the Caribbean
Land of those who endured pirates

Jamaica the little piece of Africa
The black gold in the Caribbean
Land of the fastest man on Earth
Super star athlete Usain Bolt

Jamaica the little piece of Africa
The black rock in the Caribbean
Land of Reggae super star
Bob Marley

Jamaica the little piece of Africa
The black heart in the Caribbean
Home of the Arawak's
Land of the best Ganja

Live Clean My Little Angels

Live clean my little Angels
Live wise not otherwise
Remember the Creator in the days of your youth
Be respectful to all humans
Love and appreciate Mother Earth
She has great worth
Love and appreciate Father Time
No day is guaranteed to anyone
Live clean my little Angels
Show love for each other
Be the shoulder in time of sorrow
Be the arms to embrace in happy times
Live each day like there is no tomorrow
Love to the fullest every time
Broken heart can be mend
Knowing you had a friend
Live clean my little Angels
Promise to stay close to each other
Put no one above God
Above your own flesh and blood
Give respect to get respect
Help everyone in need
Asking for nothing in return
Your reward shall come from the Creator
Pray about everything and anything
All and everything will be possible
Live clean my little Angels

Living for Jah

This life
This lifestyle
Living for Jah
This life
Filled with hope
A strong faith
With time I wait
With time I pray
This life
This life style
Living for Jah
This life
Filled with blessings
A natural high
Such oneness with Jah
Through meditations
With each waking moment I give thanks
This life
This lifestyle
Living for Jah
This life
Filled with a pure promise
Sweet salvation
Total forgiveness
Living for Jah pure and simple
The Holy Bible the guide
Filled with examples
No denying
Jah is the greatest
King of all Kings
Lord of all Lords
The great I am

In Jah I place all my trust
Oh this love I feel
Real, real oh so real
I truly believe
My soul he'll set free
This life
This lifestyle
Living for Jah

Living in Poverty

Me a try move out of poverty this year
Over 57 years I live in a poverty
To tell you the truth
Sometimes I just don't care
You see poverty it don't play fair
Poverty don't care
Poverty is a plaque
It worse than a virus
Me a move out of poverty this year
I'm packing my few belongings
Walk foot out of here
Anywhere else should be better than poverty
Well a so me hear
I got to get up and make the move this year
I'm tired to feel ashamed
Living in poverty a nightmare
You think a me alone live there
No me friends
Poverty love to share
Poverty is every where
Poverty stay day and night
All when he know that's not right
Poverty wicked it come take set
Sometimes it don't leave till you take your last breath
Only a few ever get out clear and clean
Poverty leave a scar a distinct odor
You won't look normal
You won't act normal
You become poverty
Your mind set is poverty
Your lifestyle a poverty
You know the more I think about poverty

It's the harder it gets
I'm going to try hard to forget old rass poverty
I got to make the first step
I'm going to start walk foot a morning
With my head held high
With Jah in my heart poverty and me will part
Where ever I reach and stop
I hope and I pray
Poverty will be at my back

Look How Long

Look how long we live into you all Babylon system
Look how long, look how Rass long
Look how long we suffer under you all hands
Look how long, look how Rass long
Look how long you all pretend
Look how long, look how Rass long
Look how long you all preach false doctrine
Look how long, look how Rass long
Now that Rasta see the light
We got the knowledge from the Most High
We stood up strong
We fought hard
We know it was right, these feelings we couldn't fight
Rasta is pure light, oneness and equal rights
We are in the tens of thousands strong
Rasta will forever live on
Look how long we live into you all Babylon system
Look how long, look how Rass long
Look how long you all fight we down
Look how long, look how Rass long
They gave Marcus Garvey a fight
What's in the dark must come to light
Don't call I weed head, bald heads, because you fear the Dread
Reason with I instead, knowledge you'll receive
Rasta is pure and clean
Don't judge I
I'm closer to Mother Nature than the I
Your fear is lack of knowledge of Rastafari
I am what I am
I look like my Father, come closer you'll see I powers

You don't see Rasta is taking over
All when HIS STORY showed Rasta greatness
Bob Marley had to die before half the WORLD respect his greatness
Rastafari start, it has no end, its forever
It's in one's heart
My heart is Rasta now and forever

Marcus Garvey

Of all our National Heroes
You're the one who stays on my mind
Of all our National Heroes
You're like the savor divine
Of all our National Heroes
You're sung about in more songs
We Jamaicans worship and praise your name
Some say you're a priest and prophet
I say you're more
You're a teacher, preacher, and a leader
A motivational speaker, an up-lifter, a poet
A healer and a visionary to so many
Marcus Garvey, Marcus Garvey, Marcus Garvey
You're my National Hero
Hero, Hero, Hero
My National Hero
Marcus Garvey you were the Jamaican Moses
Teaching love of self, self-worth, respect of self
For us to return to Africa our Mother land
You get plenty fight, we know it wasn't right
You said look to the East for the coming of a King
Indeed we did
Ethiopia crowned the Rasta King
And so prophesy fulfilled
Marcus Garvey, Marcus Garvcy, Marcus Garvey
You're my National Hero
Hero, Hero, Hero
My National Hero
The many confused
Body and mind abused Blacks
Eyes got opened from your uplifting powerful speeches
Body and soul were renewed

With new respect of self
Black pride became your mission
Jah gave you the vision
With all the fight, you persevered for your people
With our a doubts
You're the people's choice
Marcus Garvey you're healer, teacher our National Hero
Marcus Garvey, Marcus Garvey, Marcus Garvey
You're my National Hero
Hero, Hero, Hero
My National Hero

Master Plan

By: Chiragh Atre & Vernon Paddy

You must hold the master plan in your hands
Take a weapon bang, bang, and bang
Take an innocent brother's life
You don't even bat an eye, when you heard how his family cried
You must hold the master plan into your hands
Yes you so call leaders from all part of this land
The stroke of your pens set laws in motion
You and your advisor plan citizens' destination
You all gain our trust, get our votes
Jump onboard big yachts
Leaving us on boats
Remember it's the same tide that keeps us afloat
You must hold the master plan into your hands
Religious leaders with your fake false doctrine
Big money schemes preying on the weak
Leaching from the meek
Salvation you a preach
The Creator, Mother Nature, Fathers Time
is all we humans should seek
There is no peace to be found, it's already within ourselves
You must hold the master plan into your hands
Yes you, you same one, you know your generation
The ones who start slavery in these parts of Jah land
You all came and saw we had our own ways of life
Our own philosophies, Gods, Kings and Queens
You brain wash us kept us weak, force upon so many your blood line
Crisscross mix up mix up, mess up mess up so many minds
It's evident in today's society
So many lost souls with identity crisis
Some too brown to be full black

Some too black to feel brown
You all did hate blacks, yet you rape my great grand mother
Fulfill your sick desires
Now you burning in hell's fire
Our type was only good enough for slavery
To work on your plantations and into your factories
Yet Momma tits was good enough to suckle your white babies
Momma body was good enough to satisfy master cravings and desires
You never give us a fighting chance
You only saw the color of our skins
You knew not of the color of our thoughts
The goodness of our hearts
You just tore families apart
With the greed from your hearts
You and your money will one day depart
Lyrics a wash me like rain, cold sweat and pain
Brings inspiration to the brain
The only time we get a little ease up
Is Christmas time for their Jesus
These things get me vex and perplex
You work us like mules, treat us like fools
Give me master tear up, what left, and wear out
You come with your cross and Bible
What you think we all was just sitting back in Africa being idle
You F up History for real, only putting what
you want black people to read
You didn't see we were Kings and Queens
Pure royalty
You took us away from paradise
Now so many of us are still stuck here living in poverty
In a country that treated we like crap less than crap
Stuck in the past to Rass, to Rass, to Rass
Still stuck in mental slavery
Lost and longing for our real homes
Not sure of who we are, our real roots, our true identity lost
With time and space

Some of you bank books still fat from the blood sweat and tears
Of my great granny them backs
You know how these things get me vex
How they think we're all thugs and fools
Remember we the new Africans went to their schools
We have to find the time to re-educate our minds
Lyrics a wash me like rain, cold sweat and pain
Brings inspiration to my brain
We have to stop allowing them to play with our minds
Their brain wash education
Water down religion
Their half-truth history, that's how they trick us
They came with their crosses, plagues and diseases
Strip us of our identity
Even though they whip us
Like we were their own Pickney
We had to carry their names, oh what a Rass shame
Slavery and it F up games, just for a financial gain
Lyrics a flow like rain, cold sweat and pain
Brings inspiration to the brain

Matthew

No Matthew, no Mark, Luke or John
Could come and flop our blessed little Island
Pure prayers were sent up to the Higher Man
Jamaica was covered and protected by Jah Mighty hands

Matthew a come, Mathew a come
Maoo confuoion
Jamaicans remember Gilbert destruction
Many knees bow, many tongue confess
Praying time, praying time
Government got we a suffer enough
Jah protect we, cover we, guide we, direct we
Make Matthew bypass we
We don't need anything else to cross us
Government got that covered
Jah shield us from the wind and rain
Our hearts are filled with nuff pain
We will hold our heads high
Clean up, fix up and even pop off a smile
We Jamaicans are a resourceful kind
A bet a dollar even bawl head said a prayer
Clean heart and true Rasta's never stop burn a fire

No Matthew, no Mark, Luke or John
Could come and flop our blessed little Island
Pure prayers were sent up to the Higher Man
Jamaica was covered and protected by Jah Mighty hands

Mattie

Miss Mattie! Miss Mattie!
Look what a take place
Woman a get plenty licks
What a thing in our country
Domestic problem it's a lover's affair fe true
Call police them na help you
She live in a house with him
Him a take care of her
They have six children too
It too far gone
Come quick Miss Mattie
Fa it look like murder a go commit
Him a let off too much box and kicks
Miss Mattie! Miss Mattie!
Send fe Constable White and Sargent Brown
This look rough, this look tough
Still me na response
By this time tonight they love up, love up
While she rub up, rub up
Miss Mattie she a get nuff lick up, lick up
Still me na response
Me gone till next time Miss Mattie

Me and Corona Again

Me and Corona, me and Corona, Me and Corona again
You force up yourself like you and I are friends
You come cling on like cheap cologne
I was setting for you
I not only smell you, I felt you
Your dark evil self
Me and Corona, Me and Corona, Me and Corona again
It's not one prayers leave these lips
Corona you strong no bitch
You set up like old hurricane just a rumble the headaches
Three days straight
I never know say my body could take such a shake
Ginger tea, garlic tea, tam brine juice, lime and honey
Up my Rass self
Corona I see you love to be pampered
I had to rub up in Kalanga water
Me and Corona, Me and Corona, Me and Corona again
You try to slow me down
You try to break my spirit
Corona you buck up into the right man
My structure strong and clean
Corona you got to leave
You put up a Rass fight
I barely get any sleep at night
I truly believe I'm in the later rounds
I tell you the truth I lost count
I'm waiting for the bell to ring
I must knock you out, I will not take a decision
A dead you have to dead Corona
I'm coming out with all that I got
I'm packing my best punch
Corona when I'm done

I'm going to eat you for my breakfast and lunch
Me and Corona, Me and Corona, Me and Corona again
Fun and joke aside
If I did know I would take cover, I would have hide
Since you single out me, come and collide
This is why we are into this fight
A fight to the death
Corona how you feel to be on the losing side
You evil Rass backside
You forward, you brave, you dirty wretch
All the same, you know last week I didn't have this chat
I was on the losing end
When I remember how life sweet
I got up, stood strong, made plans to defeat Corona

Memories

Amazing how a memory never fades, amazing
how a memory never fades
It never really goes away
Good or bad, happy or sad
Memories never ever go away
Our minds rewind and replay
To remember memories that were stored away

Amazing how a memory never fades, amazing
how a memory never fades
It never really goes away
Memories of you forty years ago rewind and replay
Our text messages put it all in play
Oh! Where do we go from here?
Oh! I pray we connect and share
Making new memories along the way

Amazing how a memory never fades, amazing
how a memory never fades
It never really goes away
To the Creator I pray
Jacky for you and me to connect
Feel a good vibes and have it bless
For our love to be endless

Mind on Fire

My mind is on fire
Jah this can't be your desire
Humans are so cold
Cruelty reach new heights
Police brutality is displayed on all social Medias
My pen ablaze, my paper is in flames
I got to release this pain
It seems the news gets worse each day
Terrorist attacks
Police brutality
Rape
Murder
Mix with natural disasters seems it's all we're living for
Earth a run red too much blood shed
Prophecy did reveled man and man a go feel
My pen ablaze, my paper is in flames
Got to release this pain
Too much tears of sorrow
Too much aches and pain
Loud is the cries I hear
There is fear in the faces of our citizens
as we fight this new war for survival
To ensure they don't annihilate the Black race
Government is our new enemy
Them and their guard dogs
They brutalize us daily
While government back them up
My pen ablaze, my paper is in flames
I got to release this pain
Black lives matter
White lives matter
All lives matter

Tell me why we are so feared
Even after 400 years
Hatred and racism will always be here
America was built on rip and grab
America was built on lies and deceit
America's history lean it bend is set to suit only a few of them
We came here screaming and fighting
We will leave here doing the same
Things and time has changed but the game is the same
We will always have to fight our fight
Stand up and demand our share of this pie
There is good and bad in all races
We sometimes takes two steps forward and three steps back
but that's no reason to live in fear of being shot in the back
To be arrested unjustly
To be publicly brutalized
To die in police custody
To serve time for crimes not committed
To be falsely accused
To be disrespected
My mind is on fire
I genuinely care
I endure all these fears
I worry about my kids and what this world is becoming
My pen ablaze, my paper is in flames
I will always burn a fire
I will always speak my mind
When another hurt another human it is a crime
When our police force hurt its citizens
It's a down right disgrace and shame
Government, government
Step in, step up
We no longer a shut up
No more hush up, hush up
We are tired of turning the other cheek
We are standing up strong

We will die proud as humans
My mind is on fire
Burning hot
My pen ablaze, my paper is in flames
In flames
In flames
In flames

Mind Switch

You think a little
Roses are red violets are blue
I could write about you
All the love up love up
Stuff about you
When I think of
Old colonial rule, treating citizens like fools
White wash history that only suit certain citizens
Politics with all it tricks
Wars and all its monetary gains
Crime and all the hurting hearts
Political refugees
The many tore apart lost and living in exile
Slavery and its ugly past
Pirates who plunder stole and lived large on the Islands
Jim Crow laws that reek right here in our back yards
Civil rights with all it fights
The mind click
The subject matter get rich
That's why my tune switch
You'll never hear any
Roses are red
Violets are blue
Softy soft crap about you
Too much suffering
Too much pain
Too much lean history
So we want to set it straight
Too much brutality
Too much tears
Too much mental blocks that need to be cleared
We owe our own people the truth

We need to be fair
It's time to clear the air
We've been brainwashed by those who only saw us as fair game
Saw us as animals, puppets on their strings
The tides are changing
Watch for new waves
Our new youths are re-educating their minds
Finding the truth
We no longer will lay back
Allowing you to dish out the lashes
We're standing up, because we're fed up
We ready to fight to defend our rights
Now we've seen the light
You no longer can mess with our minds
The chains and shackles are off our arms and feet
We have cleared our minds
Our souls set free from the teachings of Marcus Garvey
Redemption songs of Bob Marley
We don't want to be treated any longer like we're less than human
We no longer going to lay back
Take your crap
Our heroes fought and die
Marcus Garvey prophecy
Bob Marley set the foundation through Reggae Music
The World has heard it
Reggae Music how can you refuse it
We the Jamaican people own it and we're not afraid to use it
To blow your minds to higher heights
We meditate and get humble thoughts
You all can't mess with us a Bumbo klaat
So when I say I'm done with
Roses are red
Violets are blue
Moon and stars crap about you
Because the subject matter is too rich
The mind already switch

So this is it
You either like it or hate it
My heart is Rasta
My thoughts are of Africa
People suffering and pain
Not of any money gain
You better walk and look over your shoulders
I'm among the many militant poets of Jah, Jah

Muhammad Ali

Of all the greats that entered the ring
Cassus Clay you and you alone win

The man named Cassus Clay
The greatest there ever was

At age 22 Cassus Clay
Changed his slave name

To the World he became
Muhammad Ali
The greatest heavy weight
Of his time
This time
And for all time

Float like a butterfly
Sting like a bee
Jah know the world
Will Mourn for Muhammad Ali

Of all the greats
That entered the ring
Muhammad Ali you had to fight outside and within

Float like a butterfly
Sting like a bee
Jah know the world
Will grieve for Muhammad Ali

You stood up strong for your rights
For what you believed in
This country and its messed up plan

Persecute you, punish you
Tried to break you
You showed the world
They couldn't rearranged you
Your new faith sustained you

Float like a butterfly
Sting like a bee
Jah know the world
Will cry for Muhammad Ali

My Angel

You will never know the big impact you have on my whole being
You light up the room when you come in
You command such greatness about you
You're my Angel sister
You touch my life in every way possible
You are such a positive force in my life
You give advice that makes sense, you're a born leader
You've guided my life from day one
You're my Angel sister
I see you, I feel you, and yes we connect
We share so much likeness, you genuinely care
You carry the world on your shoulders, you hate to let anyone down
You commit totally to people, always giving your all
You share so much kindness around
You've touched so many people
With gentle caring words and deeds
You're my Angel sister
To just know I'm apart of you, has made me a better person
You're never selfish
When angered about something or some one
You find the positives in the situation
You deserve so much more, the humble person you are
You accept and made your life bountiful enough
To be able to give to so many in need
You're my Angel sister
You will never know the big impact you have on me
You came into work every day like a beam of sun shine
I would hear your voice and close my eyes, just taking it in
Your presence warms my heart
Even on your worse hair day
You were the most beautiful in my eyes
When you cried I found somewhere to go cry too

When I knew you were feeling down, I felt for you
When you shared some happiness about, someone or something
Your eyes mirrored your heart, showing only love
You spoke only the truth
You're my Angel sister
I will never forget in my lowest low
You cared and made it possible, for me to move and be with you
You've been the mother to my kids they didn't have
Everything I have you were a part of it
You encourage people, you motivate people
You sacrifice countless for your family, you
go above and beyond the normal
So I know you live in Heaven here on Earth already
You're my angel sister
I love you

My baby

My baby is down and feeling blue
I pray the sun shines bright for you
I pray the Island warmth fills your bones
I pray the sweet sounds of reggae
Revives your soul
I pray Jah put his protective hands upon thee
Wishing I was there to hold you
Comfort you
Console you
To just simply reassure you
Of how I love and adore you
Queen

My baby is down and feeling blue
May the island breeze
Cool you down
Turn your dull feelings around
May the memories of I
Put a smile to your face
Cheer up your heart in all
The right places
Wishing I was there to hold you
Comfort you, console you
To simply reassure you
Of how I love and adore you
Queen

My Four

Sweet hugs and kisses
Soft touch
Oh how I love you four so much
Kind words
Plenty smile and laughter
Day after day
You four keep my heart beating
From all the joy I'm feeling
All the fun and play
Movies
Parties
Vacations and trips
I truly adore you four
Beautiful eyes
Gentle souls
Compassionate hearts
All that and more
Sums up my wonderful four
Jah know, Jah know
Oh how I love you four

My Girl

My girl sometimes get vex
Send me a break up text
So we can enjoy make up sex
I sometimes play along
Push the fire to fulfill her desire
She will call me a day later
With pure love into her heart
by five o'clock the two of us part
Me no take stack
Me no take check
It's just a part of her plan
To want I man back
Me and my girl share fire and ice
A type of love and hate
By the end of the day
I know she can't wait
To see I coming through the gate
The two of us just a huff and a puff
The love into our hearts just a bubble up
If you could see when we get under the sheets
How the two of us just a love up, love up
Sweet, sweet, sweet
It's the fire and ice
that makes this love so nice
Nice, nice, nice
The love and hate is how we relate
A just so we flex
My girl love make up sex

My Heart is Rasta

My heart is Rasta, my heart is Rasta
I pray to the Creator
The Creator is greater than I
I adore Mother Nature
I truly respect Fathers time
Religion is a mind set
Peace Is within everyone
Respect all other humans
Try hard to keep clean hands
Meditate and allow clear thoughts to flow
All heart is pure, men's deeds is what corrupt it
Men's deeds is the cause of all evil doings
My heart is Rasta, my heart is Rasta
Everything comes after
I will praise the highest Creator
I'm balanced in mind and body
As Rasta is pure peace
I crave more time
To enjoy this beautiful Earth
With all its wonders and splendors
I give thanks and praise for each day
The Creator is truly divine
Just look around mankind
The earth gives us all we really need
It's then men's greed that seek more than it need
This behavior leads to fuss and fights
They say craven choke puppy dog
Birds who fly too fast pass their nest
You add, multiply and divide you'll get the rest
My heart is Rasta, my heart is Rasta
With Jah love
Everything will come after

Rasta is give, Rasta don't take
You'll have to know the true from the fake
Rasta uplift, elevate and motivate
When you find true peace within
You will be closer to Jah, Jah
Be a leader not a follower
Chill, meditate close your eyes
Let your mind escape
This beautiful World has enough for all of us
Enjoy your time and space
My heart is Rasta, my heart is Rasta

My kids

Britney
I will forever love you
I will forever show you
How I care
I will be there for you always
My love will grow more with time
I knew I would and could love you endlessly
From day one Britney
You were my first special gift
So perfect
So special
I will love you always Britney
Savanna
I love you so much
My second little Princess
Ever so sweet
My love will also grow more with time
For you Savanna
You were a special gift to me
So perfect
So special
So dear to me
I will love you always Savanna

My Pen Ablaze

My pen ablaze
It ablaze
It ablaze
It ablaze
It ablaze for the rest of my days
Lyrics hot and a flow from my brain
My paper is in flames
It can't contain
The information got me going insane
Can't take what's going on in society
All the cruelty
Police brutality
The amount of mistaken identity
Citizen a suffer
Black people dying by the hour
We are at war with the government
they need to control who them a send
come protect and serve us
more like come to kill us
My pen ablaze
It ablaze
It ablaze
It ablaze
It ablaze for the rest of my days
Lyrics hot and a flow from my brain
My paper in in flames
In flames
In flames
In flames
It can't contain
The information got me going insane
Can't take what's going on in society

The media can't keep up with all the madness
Human minds can't register all the sadness
It's not right
It can't be ok
Police are killing and destroying us each day
Government step in
Government step up
Start to train up, or you will never be able to correct
All the F-ups
My pen ablaze
It ablaze, it ablaze, it ablaze
It ablaze for the rest of my days
Lyrics hot and a flow from my brain
my paper is in flames, in flames, in flames, in flames

My Pets

By: Britney Paddy & Vernon Paddy

China thanks for a beautiful year
I saw in the kid's eyes how they cared
We all cried when you went to Doggy Heaven

Goofy you came and captivated our hearts
Goofy you were such a treat
All you did was eat, eat and eat
Bulk you up was the order of each day
In three second flat your pan was clean
Wonder why you left
After the first week we knew
Goofy never again we'll see your sweet face

Opal my sweet little baby
What a treat, what a treat
Oh how I loved your sweet little feet
When you stood up for the first time
The love for you went high up
You came and captivate, motivate, elevate and gave
When you was at your last, I held you soft
Knew it had to be, heaven needed you sweet little Oppy

Suki my most wonderful girl
Eight years and the many magical memories can't be erased
Daddy love you Suki
Now you bring such joy to CJ's heart

Topaz you're the only one
Topaz you may well be the last one to share my heart
For Topaz I know one day we'll have to part
Till then my sweet little man
Daddy love you Topy

New Day New Vibes

New day, new vibes, new reasons to survive this life
So I stay in forever contact with Jah Jah
Speaking out aloud my mind
Pleading to Jah Jah in prayers
Asking for extra strength, guidance, protection
For mankind to change their wicked ways
To make that transition to see new lights
Following what's right
For mankind to see and respect this sweet life
Protecting their souls
For the wheel of evil forever keeps turning
New day, new vibes, new reasons to survive this life
So I stay in forever contact with Jah Jah
Speaking out aloud my mind
Pleading to Jah Jah in prayers
I see men living, I see men dying
With time ticking, ticking away
Sweet precious time
Act now don't wait
Redemption may be too late
Salvation is free
Jah Jah is for all of us
New day, new vibes, new reasons to survive this life
So I stay in forever contact with Jah Jah
Speaking out aloud my mind
Pleading to Jah Jah in prayers
I see earth a run dread
Too much blood shed
Find what works for you, you, you and you
Sow good seeds and reap great rewards
Keep humble thoughts
So you and Jah Jah will never part

Keep Jah Jah close
Keep Jah Jah in your hearts
The reward in life everlasting
New day, new vibes, new reasons to survive this life
So I stay in forever contact with Jah Jah
Speaking out aloud my mind
Pleading to Jah Jah in prayers
For mankind to find Jah Jah
Oh find Jah Jah, oh find Jah Jah

No Matter

No matter your ideology
No matter your philosophy
No matter your ethnicity
No matter your religious beliefs

Remember you a human and a blood run through your veins
Remember you a human and a blood run through your veins

Obey the Ten Commandments sent from Jah above
Respect the laws of the land set by fellow humans

No matter your education
No matter your wealth

Remember you a human and a blood run through your veins
Remember you a human and a blood run through your veins

Respect yourselves
Respect your brothers and sisters

No matter your gender
As long as we are obedient to the Father

Remember you a human and a blood run through your veins
Remember you a human and a blood run through your veins

No Problem

Jamaicans say no problem
No problem, no problem, no problem
A lie, a lie, a lie them a tell, a lie, a lie, a lie them a tell
We have Nuff problems
Nuff problems, Nuff problems
Make us start with the Rass government
The Rass government
They're holding us back
They're keeping us in darkness
When we want to see the light and live up right
In a Jah Jah sight
In a Jah Jah sight, in a Jah Jah sight
Jamaicans say no problem
No problem, no problem, no problem
A lie, a lie, a lie them a tell, a lie, a lie, a lie them a tell
We have Nuff problems
Nuff problems, Nuff problems
Make we start with the foreign press
They publish Nuff false information
For us to look the worst when we're trying our best
To scrape through life's situations and deal with our own stress
They need to deal with their own crap and mess
War, crime, murder and violence have been
around since the start of civilization
They crucify Jesus Christ and that's a fact
You remember that
Jamaicans say no problem
No problem, no problem, no problem
A lie, a lie, a lie them a tell, a lie, a lie, a lie them a tell
We have Nuff problems
Nuff problems, Nuff problems
Make we start with homelessness

How the Rass we a go clean up that dirty mess
That dutty mess, that dutty mess
Government, leaders, world preachers
Promoting this, promoting that
While poor people living in shit and crap
So so shit and crap, so so shit and crap
With no food to put in their pots
You want me to keep on chatting
For us all to chat, chat and chat
Before you all do something about that
Jamaicans say no problem
No problem, no problem, no problem
A lie, a lie, a lie them a tell, a lie, a lie, a lie them a tell
We have Nuff problems
Nuff problems, Nuff problems
Make us start with the Jamaica Defense Force
And the Jamaica Police Department
Some who a terrorize their own people very soul
A Nuff they send gone take rest
Not sleep
Permanent rest, permanent rest
Corruption wreak every part of our cities
Oh Jah what a pity, human minds so iffy
Human minds so filled with greed and envy
Jamaicans say no problem
No problem, no problem, no problem
A lie, a lie, a lie them a tell, a lie, a lie, a lie them a tell
We have Nuff problems
Nuff problems, Nuff problems
Make we start with history
History, her story, my story, your story
Slavery
Yes, yes, yes slavery
We were in Africa a satta nice and easy, nice and easy
They carry us away in captivity
They know themselves, they and them greedy great grand parents

And require from us our blood, sweat and
tears for over four hundred years
Fire bun, fire bun, fire bun
A now you want to care
You better start divvy up and share
Land, silver, gold and a mule
You think all Black people a fool, you think
we a go sit back and just cool
We have been educated
Me not preaching prejudice so don't get I wrong
This is for all who aren't doing the right
Not doing right, not doing right
Me a beg you all to free up your minds
Follow laws and treat others right
Jamaica it's time we realize the powers Jah have fallen on the I
The I and the I them
We all have the power to change
The power to rearrange
We can care and learn how to share
To live our lives without fears
No more tears
Unless its tears of joy
From east to west
From north to south
Oh Jah you hear how I a shout
Jamaicans need to walk a new route

Off The Deep Edge

From the depth of Holy Hell
I walk alone
Struggling fussing
With my inner thoughts
Cursing out loud
With mixed emotions
Deep within the bottomless pit
In total darkness
Lost amongst the dead souls in Holy Hell
I ponder all the what ifs
What if I did this differently?
What if I did that differently?
Trap in Holy Hell heat
An everlasting torment
Suffering endlessly
With no control or say
There is nothing I can do to avoid Holy Hell
Break free to get away
To run to escape this darkness of Holy Hell
The thick intense smog in Holy Hell
The air is limited in Holy Hell
It hurts to breathe
Seconds in Holy Hell seems like days
You're confronted with all and every fears
Everyone around is in total confusion
Fussing and cussing
Fighting and killing
Death becomes a wish
Words can't express the terror of Holy Hell
The torture
The mental abuse
The physical strength to just endure this one moment in Holy Hell

Oh Sandy, oh Sandy

Who would ever think little old Sandy
Could a brush Jamaica, pass through Cuba and Haiti
Pick up steam and come to America
Sandy you ambitious
Oh Sandy, oh Sandy, oh, oh Sandy, look what you do to we
Oh Sandy, oh Sandy, oh, oh Sandy, look what you do to we
Why you never miss us, why you never pass we
Look how you left us in such agony, in such agony
What a time you take to come right before election
Put a damper in we plans mess up we lives
We barely got over Katrina now we back on our knees
Shouts and cries to the Lord
Oh Sandy, oh Sandy, oh, oh Sandy, look what you do to we
Oh Sandy, oh Sandy, oh, oh Sandy, look what you do to we
Why you never miss us, why you never pass we
Look how you left us in such agony, in such agony
Exodus tells of the movement of Jah people
Scattered and displaced
Revelation reveals it
Man and man a go feel it
A time to get wise or be otherwise
We need to respect Mother Nature
We need to enjoy Father Time
Global warning in full effect
Earth is being put to the test
We not even feel the full wrath yet
Oh Sandy, oh Sandy, oh, oh Sandy, look what you do to we
Oh Sandy, oh Sandy, oh, oh Sandy, look what you do to we
Why you never miss us, why you never pass we
Look how you left us in such agony, in such agony
Sandy you vicious

Olympics

In the pool Michael Phelps rules
The brother makes swimming look cool
On the tracks Bolt a the man that
A the man that, A the man that
Bolt run and smile happy all the time
The rest huffing and puffing
When Bolt done with them
It's as if their guts bursting
Read their lips
They all are cursing
Bolt beat them with a smile
Even when he start slow
Giving them a glimpse of hope
The end results show
He's the fastest man on earth
Jah know
Bolt beat them with a smile
Then puts on a show for the crowd
Pride and power
Jamaica celebrates
Thompson elevates
The baton has pass
A new Queen on the throne
Thompson bringing home the Gold
Hoosiers pride our Athletes
Coming home on high
Simone Biles pure power and positive Vibes
Simone Manuel moves us forward
from a place of shame and disgrace
from darkness to the bright lights
Pride up, pride up
Jah sees how we're great

This Rio Olympics we have a lot to celebrate
Emotions on high
We saw joyous tears
The stories heard, seen and shared
We saw blood, sweat and tears
Athletes overcoming trials and tribulations
Giving of themselves their all and then some
Sorrow and pain
Disappointment and fears
Happiness as those victorious celebrates
Champions graceful in defeat congratulating
the new holders of that feat
Laughter and smiles
Old records broken as new ones were set
This Rio Olympics was simply the best

On high

You sit up on high, a pass your judgement
Pass your judgement and you know it's not right
You know it's not right
You don't remember the only one that paid the ultimate price
Jehovah
So kibba your mouth, and all your bitter comments
Your hurtful remarks spark
Pain and violence, pain and violence, pain and violence
Loose lips sink ships
You sit up on high, an enjoy the good life
Smoking expensive cigars, drinking fine champagne and wines
Eating food of your choice, how nice
You ever stop! Think once or twice
Of your fellow brother man, and his lifestyle
Flip the coin, flip the script, it could be you living in the streets
Hustling, bustling to make ends meet
You live your life say it sweet
You ever consider the man in the streets
What about his basic needs, the things you take for granted
The many days you waste, he can only dream of the taste
Dream of the taste, dream of the taste, dream of the taste
Money the root of all evil
You sit up on high, a glare and a stare, without a conscience
You never struggle to pay your rent
He's living outdoors facing all the elements
And is at risk for all violence
You see from your eyes but it doesn't register to your heart
You see but you turn a blind eye
It doesn't register to your heart for you to be a part of this
That is much greater than you
Much greater than you, much greater than you, much greater than you
Be compassionate be kind

Give to the poor from what you have in store
Give with a cheerful heart, you and Jah will never part
For now Jah dwells into your heart
"Blessed are those who hunger and thirst for righteousness"
Now you see the light humble and be meek like a child
A chapter a day keeps the devil away, so get on your knees and pray
Now you see the light, I hope you'll stand up and fight this good fight
Eliminating, hunger, poverty, homelessness and violence
Lend a helping hand to those less fortunate than yourself
The Father sits on high, he is watching you
Do good and good will follow you

Pass Me The Pen and The Paper

Pass me the pen and the paper
Pass me the pen and the paper
Pass me the pen and the paper
This one can't stay till later
I have to write this one down me brothers
2 types of justice America
Pass me the pen and the paper
Pass me the pen and the paper
Pass me the pen and the paper
My brain is on fire
It's a burning desire
Time to call out the old bag of liars
2 types of justice America
Pass me the pen and the paper
Pass me the pen and the paper
Pass me the pen and the paper
Too many died on these soils of America
The earth is blood soaked
It reeks, it stinks
Innocent Blacks Browns souls
Have been taken by the deadly forces
2 types of justice America
Built on pure envy, hate, corruption and greed
Blacks and Browns have suffered the most
From orders coming down from the elites
Deadly justice dealt out by hands of corrupted cops
America has been running red hot
We have taken the number one spot
Corruption from the tip top
All they care about is that their money stack
Most of their woman love Brown and Black
Years and years of their evil plan has been set back

To wipe out the Browns and Blacks
Their grandsons and daughters are shades of Brown and Black
Many reject them that's a fact
Pass me the pen and the paper
Pass me the pen and the paper
Pass me the pen and the paper
This one a fire

Where Were You

Where were you when me a
Pick up junk, pick up junk, pick up junk
Where were you when me a
Pick up junk
Where were you, where were you
Now you step up front
Take man for a punk
A smile and reap
From all my sweet
Take you self around the back
And stay there, stay there, stay there
Me work hard all day in the sun and heat
To make sure my family eat
Cream rise to the top
Stars shine brightly
You're neither or either
That's a fact
Where were you when me a
Pick up junk, pick up junk, pick up junk
Where were you when me a
Pick up junk
Where were you, where were you, where were you
Now you step up front
Take man for a punk
You don't like to get your hands dirty
So how you think you're worthy
You're grabbing and reaching always begging
Take you self around the back
And stay there, stay there, stay there

Me work hard all day in the rain and cold
To make sure my family eat
Cream rise to the top
Stars shine brightly
You're neither or either
That's a fact

Political Aspiration

You and your political aspiration
Greed is your only desire
Your motivation is the $ sign
You are spitting fire
You talk the talk
You walk the walk
Seeking votes
Seeking power
Now you're at the tip top
I hear you talking all that crap
You easily forget your promises
Oh they were lies!
You pretend to be wise now we see you otherwise
You and your political aspiration
Leadership is on your mind
Its takes a certain type
To keep the people in mind
You talk the talk
You walk the walk
You spark fire
Made all those promises
We see you
You riding high
You up up tight
Nothing about you is right
We the people will always fight
You lined your pockets
With silver and gold
Remember we all get feeble and old
The better parts of your story will never be told
When you should live your life helping people all the time
You live flossy

You live glossy
All that glitters is not gold
A fool and his money
Jah know it's funny
You and your political aspirations
You steering in the wrong direction
You're on a collision course
You will flip and flop
You will get off track
Karma will come full circle that is certain

Poor Man Struggle

Poor man struggle, poor man struggle
See my Black brother a walk the beach collecting bottles
Poor man struggle, poor man struggle
Man with heavy load
Click and clack the noise of the bottles
Poor man struggle, poor man struggle
See my Black brothers and sisters
Juggling to beat the system
Never to get ahead
To survive and live or to cash it in and die
There is no other way
You better follow this rough route
Jah the system dread, dread it dread
Government a dig out the little
Dig out, dig out, dig out and dig out
Them stop dig out yet?
NO
Poor man struggle, poor man struggle

Pride & Power

By: Mia Atre & Vernon Paddy

Black man's power
Black man's pride
Step up don't stay behind
You see what Usain Bolt
Done for our little Island
Shelly-Ann Fraizer Price takes all the top prizes
V. C. Brown done made us proud
Black man's power
Black man's pride
Step up, step up don't stay behind
Let's not forget
Donald Quarry, and sweet Merlene Otty oh she a Queen
Arthur Wint, Lennox Miller, George Rhoden,
Herb McKinley and Leslie Laing
They're all Olympians
Black man's power
Black man's pride
Step up, step up, step up don't stay behind
Respect to the late great heavy weight Trevor Berbeck
Oh Shrimpy Clark too
I want to big up Richard Hall and Owen Beck
From the fist of fire Negril crew
Black man's power
Black man's pride
Step up don't stay behind
The Wailing Wailers conquer the four corners
Our musical ambassador
Gregory Isaacs the cool ruler
Dennis Brown the Crown Prince
John Holt the man with the 1000 volts

Black man's power
Black man's pride
Step up, step up don't stay behind
Jimmy Cliff with guns ablaze set the movie craze
Paul Campbell super shine on the silver screen
I feel the power, I swell with pure pride
Keep stepping up don't stay behind
Black man's power
Black man's pride
Step up, step up, step up don't stay behind
Big them up, Miss Lou and Maso Ron
They were two of our first comedian
Blacka Ellis
Itchy and Fancy Cat
Oliver Samuel, would kill you with laughter
A plenty young Jamaican
A follow these great trend setters
We big in the arts
Reggae music and Jamaica can't part
Sweet Ganja me love it to my heart
White Rum a nuff times it lick me down
Oh Jamaican oh Jamaican
I feel the power, I swell with pride
Keep stepping up don't stay behind
Wait! What you're saying my brother, don't forget
Freddie Martin, Karl Nunes, Chris Gayle,
Courtney Walsh and Michael Holding
These men are our Cricket God Fathers

Pure Stress

Don't worry what I make
There is none for you to take
I have a lot at stake
Wake from your sleep and slumber
I finally got your number
Craven choke puppy dog
You too greedy, you too greedy
Always so needy
So needy, so needy
Don't watch what I'm doing
Get your own house in order
I'm going to burn a fire for you
Now I know you're fake
Your cake done bake
Not a slice more you a take
You too greedy, you too greedy
Always so needy
So needy, so needy
Don't study I no more
I done calculate
I have dot the I's cross my T's
See you for what you are
It's not my desire
So I have to burn this fire
Puff up like smoke
You're a bag a joke
Can't take I for granted any more
I won't live in your fantasy
I sight the reality
You too greedy, you too greedy
Always so needy
So needy, so needy

Don't worry
I'll get through this with the help from Jah, Jah
Oh how I sight your evil plans
Saw your true colors
Your intentions was to kill and destroy
You was going to take me for a toy
Your boy a yard
Karma came full circle
You know you've mess up
I can forgive, I just can't forget
That's why I'm leaving
You're no longer appealing
You too greedy, you too greedy
Always so needy, so needy, so needy

Puss

By: Jadah Li & Vernon Paddy

Love the, love the, love the little puss
Love the, love the, love the black puss
Love the, love the, love the big puss
Little puss, big puss, black puss, white puss
Love puss, love puss, love puss
Love puss, love puss, love the puss
Love the, love the, love the pretty little puss
Love the, love the, love the pretty black puss
Love the, love the, love the pretty big puss
Little puss, big puss, black puss, white puss
Love puss, love puss, love puss
Love puss, love puss love the puss
Love the puss, love the puss
The puss, the puss, the puss
From Brownsburg bush
Yes the puss, yes the puss
Yes the bush puss
Run outside puss
Nyam the others food puss
Climb the tree puss
Sleep pon the bed puss
Little puss, big puss black puss, white puss
The one Savanna find into Brownsburg bush
Pretty, pretty Barbie Puss

Rasta Light

Now I see the light, the light that shines so bright
Now I see the light, the true and everlasting light
The light about Rastafari
I'm no longer into the dark
No chains can bound me
No mental chains can enslave me
I'm free, I'm free
Knowledge of Jah set me free
Knowledge of self I'm now free
Babylon can no longer school I
Their history lean it bend it and I was never friends
Babylon system can no longer hold I down
I know where Jah is leading I
I know my self-worth, I am no longer just I
I'm a child of the Most High King
I carry Jah within
They don't like to see us win
That's why they rewrite and rearrange every thing
Hid the truth about our original Kings and Queens
Set it so they look like the king
Trust me what was hidden into the darkness
must come out into the light
You know how long we a fight
For Babylon to see that Rasta is right
Rasta is pure righteousness, Rasta is true peace within
Rasta's is the children of the Everlasting King Jah
Now I see the light, the light that shines so bright
Now I see the light, the true and everlasting light
The light about Rastafari
I can see the clear path
Their chains and shackles are broken
The powers of Jah uplift I

I'm free, I'm free
Knowledge of Jah set me free
Knowledge of self I'm now free
All that they taught I, was only to fool me
Trap I, enslave I
to keep I into the darkness, to mess with I mind
Babylon system can no longer confuse I
Jah words is the lamp light that shines to lead I
Jah words is the pure energy
Jah words is the levity
Jah words is from creation
I'm no longer just I
I'm a child of the Most High King
I carry Jah within

Rivers to Cross

By: Mia Atre & Vernon Paddy

The many rivers to cross
Each man burden seems the heaviest
Yet no man knows his hour
The Mighty Creator
He gives and he takes
Awake, rise, keep your eyes on the prize
No time to stumble or fumble
Walk humble stay on the straight and narrow
You'll live to see tomorrow
The many rivers to cross
Good friends you have
Those you have lost
Memories of the past
will forever stay with you
Till your time pass
Human lives entwine, cross, collide and mix
A blend of energy that creates history
You and that person's story
As we live we travel in time
Moving forward with time
The mind is the only part of the human
That can go back into the past
Relive a memory
Human life is a ticking clock
That one day will stop
The many rivers to cross
It's how we cleanse, clean, and wash away the old self
Taking on a new attitude
A new mind set, new in how we think
Finding inner peace for each tribulation

183

Showing the strength to overcome trials
The many rivers to cross
During a life span
Leaving behind the old
Stepping into the future each second
With time, in time, using time

Running and Running

Running and running
You're running away
But you can't run away from yourself
No rock or hole will be too big or deep for you to hide
Our patriot missiles will seek and find
Running and running
You're running away
But you can't run away from Jah Jah
One little man causing such destruction on the land
You know when we get you the cuffs will be on your hands
Running and running
You're running away
But you can't run away from the truth
Pack up now
Just leave
Enough tears have been wept
Stop! Smell the roses
Acknowledge the facts
We've launch our attack
There is no turning back
Running and running
You're running away
But you can't run away this time
How many more have to die?
So much pain and cries
Blood sweat and tears
Suffering is everywhere
You a terror
Terror no more
Here is the truth
The boys in blue will get to you
A whole country under your tight grip

Your grip is about to slip
You surely going to feel the whip
Your time is here your end is near
Our boys wear the flag of freedom
Our pledge to defeat
We're born No fear
I hope the whole rass of you all can hear
From your caves and rock holes
We will dig and explore
Your names are on a bullet
Our boy going to pull it
You're running and you're running away
There will be nowhere to hide this time

Sake of Corona

Sake of Corona I can't have any sex
Sake of Corona I can't have any sex
Jah know star I man vex
My girl in isolation
Everyday It's just text, text, text
I'm tired of all this phone sex

Sake of Corona I can't kiss my girl
Sake of Corona I can't kiss my girl
You have to be checking for Corona breath
For that would be the kiss of death

Sake of Corona I can't hug my girl
Sake of Corona I can't hug my girl
This social distancing is a curse
I don't know between it and Corona who is the worse

Savanna

Savanna
How much I love you
The trust I place in you
The pride I feel when I see you
The high expectations I have for you

Savanna
Oh how I love you so
The inner beauty you possess
Your outer beauty shines
Your happy every day style
Oh never change being you

Savanna
How much I love you
That laughter, your smile
Your brown eyes like mines
Sparkle with life
Know I care about everything you do, say, feel
Come to me first, I will always be there for you
I will always care

Savanna
Oh how I love you so
You're an angel
You're a star
You're goodness
You can reach greatness
You can do any and everything you desire

Savanna
How much I love you
Never forget your Lord
He loves you too
Give more that you get
Show love to all
Keep being you, sweet, soft, special, and unique, irie, and smart
My baby
Savanna

Searching for The Taliban

Searching for the Taliban
Along a river so long
Against all odds
We're in a foreign land
We're all legal bounty hunters
Hungry for a capture
Dead or alive
We got to survive
Spirits are kept high
From day till night
Days spent marching
Enduring the intense heat of the sun
The deadly sand storms
My nights spent marching
On to victory
Against all odds
Our mission on hand
Iraqi freedom
Iraqi freedom
Terrorism no more
Dictator dictate your last
We're coming for your rass
Equal rights for all
Peace and love throughout all lands
We don't need to fire any weapons
Every man with a common plan
To treasure and cherish life
To respect time and space
We all live on Earth
Let's know our worth

Some People or Those People

People see but act blind to all the wonders and signs
They hear the cries of others but act deaf
All humans share Earth
For some race it's just an open range prison
For some race its total paradise, everything nice
What is freedom for some is modern day slavery for many
Slavery still exist, with a new twist, modernized to suit society
Lives have been rearranged but nothing has changed
You ever wonder how parts of this World hold the richest resources
Yet their citizens are the poorest
The haves and the have nots
The uptown and the downtown
Division, dividing human beings, classes between all races
The privilege and the underprivileged
The rich and the poor, beggar man and the thief
Those who cry and those who makes others cry
The truth vs. the lie
World history is a horror story
Puss and dog don't have the same luck
You know the one that get F up
Some stay lucky, some run out of luck
Your see no evil, speak no evil, hear no evil mentality
Must stop to Rass, to Rass, to Rass
While your brothers suffer, cry and die daily
While your sisters struggle, hustle and turn tricks to survive
You'll be the first to pass your judgement
You hypocrites don't draw my tongue
Your day is coming, you'll stumble and fall
Karma is a witch, that bitch who rides the horse of your dirty past
What you did in the dark, now coming out into the light
You think two wrong makes a right?
Should we turn the next cheek?

Should any human act that weak?
Religion is what we seek for any inner peace
Who really know what's right from what's wrong?
All human should seek till they fine what feels right
All humans are individuals, unique, one of
a kind, with their own minds
Never mute, never be silent, speak your minds
Fight for equal rights and justice
Peace is within every humans
Speak your minds, know your worth, love self, love others
Respect Mother Nature, appreciate Father Time
With every breath you take, live real, and never be a fake
No time to sleep, be awake
Be among those lucky few who choose to open
Their eyes, ears and mouth to the suffering of others

Speak Your Mind

By: Mia Atre & Vernon Paddy

Speak your mind child, speak your mind
You're a child of the king on high
Speak your mind child, speak your mind
No weapons form against you shall prosper
You utter praises to the Heavenly Father
Speak your mind child, speak your mind
You're a child of the king on high
Speak your mind child, speak your mind
Never silent, never mute
Open your mouth you speak the truth
Show no fear of these brutes
Your clean hands, your pure heart, you and Jah can't part
Speak your mind child, speak you mind
You're a child of the king on high
Speak your mind child, speak your mind
Defending justice, demanding equal rights
Peace is a state of mind, meditate you'll find yours
The words was from the beginning, the words will be there till the end
Good will conquer evil every time
Might can't beat rights, when Jah is by your side
Speak your mind child, speak your mind
You're a child of the king on high
Speak your mind child, speak your mind
Words when used correctly can be so effective
Against negative elements
Words can break down barriers, words can make men humble
Words can drive away fears, allowing men to fly away
Words can block out evil thoughts
Words can open the eyes of those blinded
By prejudice against another human

———

Speak your mind child, speak your mind
Speak it all the time, speak loud, speak clear
A Jah we fear
Speak loud, speak clear, let your works be seen
Some will agree, some will disagree
You're defending your freedom of speech
Stand firm, don't bend, and don't lean
No silence, no mute, keep speaking the truth
Speak your mind child, speak your mind
You're a child of the king on high
Speak you mind child, speak your mind
Words are vibrations
Loud enough vibrations can shake a foundation
Can fine it way in the hearts of men
Change enemy to friend
Change weakness to strength
Less to more, poor to riches
From low to high
Words can open eyes
Can clear bad minds
Speak your mind, speak your mind
Speak your mind, speak your mind

Spoken words

I'm a Jah bless vocal warrior
I am ready to chant down all oppressors with lyrics
Clean conscious precise words will flow like a river
Flow like rain in summer
Ears will listen, hearts will change
Eyes will open to see new light
New truth from words spoken
Men, women and child will follow new paths
To greater and better places in their lives
I and I a Jah bless messenger only doing Jah works
My words are pure and clean
My words teach peace, love and togetherness
My words armed with force to change one's mind
I will not be silent not now not ever
Let clean lyrics flow to show that I'm close to Jah oneness
I only deliver, never a taker
I am the giver of words, spoken words
To make positive changes for the future, for all wellbeing
I see no color, I see each as one, all men as equal
I will preach words of righteousness
Words from the scripture
I will speak frankly
I will speak openly
Words soft, easy and yet effective with its message
You will feel the power, you will see the light
Of new vibes from pure words
Clean and clear like the springs from Jah Earth that flows
To help life flourish for all mankind
Cooling and quenching every man's heart with words
Pure words, simple words
I and I a Jah vocal warrior
Don't anger me, my words will only get stronger

My words are like the calm before the storm easy with warning
My lyrics tear down all barriers
Take heed and listen
Men got to change from their wicked ways
It's never too late to see new vibes
Walk new paths, speak new words
Clean and clear
Uplifting and encouraging others
From
Yes
Spoken words

Spy game

Government a watch we! Government a watch we!
They don't even deny the lie
Government hush, hush up the truth
We a watch them a watch we
Two can play the same game
It's not now government a watch we
For years them a play spy game
No branch of government want to take the blame
Now the truth get leak
Why is man so weak?
Needy and ever so greedy
Answers citizens a seek
We a watch them a watch we
Two can play the same game
I will not call any names
We know who the biggest culprits in the game
So why them a finger point the blame
Them all guilty it's a shame
Shame! Shame! Shame!
We a watch them a watch we
Two can play the same game
Government a watch we! Government a watch we!
Now the truth get leak
Answers the whole Rass a them a seek
Name calling finger pointing to not look too weak
Redemption they all have to seek
Time to clean up their dirty mess
And put this to rest
Don't think citizens will ever forget
Government and their spy games

Still I Rise Up

Still I rise up
After all your lies
Still I rise up
After years of your verbal abuse
Still I rise up
After all I've been accused of by you
Still I rise up
As I rose up I had to fight
Had to overcome your chains and shackles
That you placed on me
The control
Mind and body abuse
Still I rise up
After years of brain washing
Tongue lashing
Gender and race bashing
Still I rise up, still I rise up
A new me wash clean and free

Still I Rise

Still I rise
When you try to kill I with cut eye
Still I rise
Even when you never stop from telling so-so lies
Still I rise
When you show envy and hate towards I
Still I rise
When you fight against Rastafari
Still I rise
Still I rise
Still I rise
When you pass your judgement upon I
Due to your lack of knowledge and understanding
of Haile Selassie
I represent the Power of the Trinity
I respect the Right Excellent Marcus Mosiah Garvey
I is Rasta
I is the Light
I represent truth and rights
I is Peace
I is the Voice
I is the people's choice
I is one of Jah Jah children
Still I rise
Still I rise
Still I rise
When you brutalize my brothers and sisters
Create your society to look down upon Rasta followers
Still I rise
When you discriminate against Rastafari
Still I rise
With all your prejudice against I

———

Still I rise
Still I rise
Still I rise
I is Rasta
I is the Light
I represent truth and rights
I is Peace
I is the example of Jah Jah
Rasta is the only choice
Still I rise
Still I rise
Still I rise

Story Time

Don't trust no shadow after dark
A beg you walk fast and pass
The youth's minds are so cold
Last week a nuff youths them put on froze
A no story I am telling
Even the blind can see we're into end time
Into end time, into end time
Men hearts so cold, men heart so bold
Men thoughts so dark
Careful how you talk
Bush have ears
Loose lips sink ships
A no story I am telling
Know your friends different from your enemy
They will laugh up in your face
Behind your back a so so disgrace
To get you out of your place
Every day above ground is to be praised
Don't live your life into a daze
Weak minds we get you crazy
A no story I am telling
A beg you see and blind
Hear and deaf
Them a youths no take check
If a revenge you a seek
There is no reward to get
You going to stumble, fumble and get left behind
Them no ramp to put you into end time
Into end time, into end time
A no story I am telling
I am not going to put my voice on pause
Me a fight this great cause

I am not going to put my vibes on mute
I am going to tell it like it is
These youths a run it like old brutes
They don't care who them brush
It must give them a rush a kind of high
A send people to meet Jah in the sky
A no story I am telling

Sweet Sweet Jamaica

Sweet sweet Jamaica my colorful people
Sweet sweet Jamaica my colorful people
I hold my head to the sky in prayers
Oh Jah we need you now, not later
We a suffer, we a suffer ya
Too much iffy-ness, too much shitty-ness
Jamaica need to be bless, to be bless, to be bless
Sweet sweet Jamaica my colorful people
Sweet sweet Jamaica my colorful people
Political crisis we need to fix it
War and crime a blow poor people minds
Too much a get early rest
Too much get perfect peace
Too much suffering out in the streets
It's a deadly battle field
We need to clean up our streets, clean up
our streets, clean up our streets
Sweet sweet Jamaica my colorful people
Sweet sweet Jamaica my colorful people
I hold my head to the sky in prayers
Oh Jah we need you now, not later now!
Poor people tears flow like river
Too much blood spill in our streets
I hear the cries, I hear the cries
Mothers bawl, fathers bawl, brothers bawl, sisters bawl
Our citizens is at war amongst each other
Human sacrifice another brother just died
Human sacrifice for politics Oh Jah why
Human sacrifice listen to the government lies
Sweet sweet Jamaica my colorful people
Sweet sweet Jamaica my colorful people
Heads of government things out of control

Too much hungry bellies a growl
Mothers hungry, fathers hungry, youths hungry
I can't lie
And you wonder how crime is at an all-time high
Poverty reeks, poverty reeks
Things smell shitty, things smell shitty
Oh Jah what a pity, what a pity
This can't be our destiny
Our little rock a crumble under the weight
of political mismanagement
Sweet sweet Jamaica my colorful people
Sweet sweet Jamaica my colorful people
I hold my head to the sky in prayers
Calling on the most high Father
Oh Jah we need you now, not later
Jah we need you now, Jah we need you now
Oh Jah, Jamaica need you now

Switch

Switch, switch, I heard you switch
now you know that I'm rich
You're singing a new tune
now you hear I'm rich
I used to treasure dimes and pennies
now I'm enjoying expensive cigars, champagne
and fine wines
Switch, switch, I heard you switch
now you know that I'm rich
You're singing a new tune
now you hear I'm rich
Girls like you come dime a dozen
I'm surrounded by super-hot chicks
Super fine honeys
Who don't need me for my money
Switch, switch, I heard you switch
now you know that I'm rich
You singing a new tune
now you hear I'm rich
I used to live in the ghetto
Now I live in the Meadows
Now my papers are stack
you think you can just come back
It don't work like that
You got to earn your spot back
You've been replaced, you've been erased
Deleted
End of the game
You want my fortune and to share in my fame
You got to be more than a pretty face
Switch, switch, I heard you switch
now you know that I'm rich

You singing a new tune
now you hear I'm rich
You better head on down that lonely track
head on down to where you were at
I'm not going there, not going to play that
You're yesterday's news
you're old and used
I'm current like time
I'm one step ahead of the pack
I told you my papers are stack
I don't need no more crap

System Set a Way

The system set a way
Set a way
It has rules but it's not a game
The system set a way
Set a way
The system set by the Man
Divide and rule was its only plan
We grew in numbers
many releasing the mental and physical chains that the system set
We grew in numbers
Many reeducating and standing up for the causes dear to our race
We are now feared in new ways
The system says we have rights
Rights we can exercise
We use our voices demanding equality and justice each day
We grew in numbers
We fought and died alongside our fellow citizens in all their wars
We are still fighting
We are still dying
To preserve our Black Race
The system set by the Man
Instill fear and disgrace was the new plan
We grew in numbers
The great Marcus Garvey
Preached and taught so many to rise up
To respect and love self
To find the truth and recognize the lies
We grew in numbers, we stood up tall
Many questioned their origins
Many found new vibes in realizing their greatness
The system set by the Man
The new plan was to kill, destroy, and humiliate the Black Race

We grew in numbers
The great Martin Luther King Jr
Beseeched us to use peace and love
To march and protest for our equal rights
The system murdered and mutilated
Too many citizens of the Black Race
we grew in numbers
We rose above the cruel system
We have never stopped fighting
We just want to be recognized
To be accepted, to enjoy equal rights
To live like citizens of this country
To be seen as Humans of Earth
To be accepted as beautiful people of the Black Race

Take Heed

Children handling adult content
Larking the maturity to deal with the consequences
Desperation on the rise, kids pushed to be grown
Behavior out of control
Drugs using body abusing mind wasting
Society lost society lost
To Rass to Rass
Homelessness affects so many
It knows no prejudice
The young the old, you, me
White and black
We take two steps forward, and one step back
Desperation on the rise
The haves and have-nots
Crime on the rise
Inflation reek our cities
Oh Jah what a pity
Man and man a live so iffy
If I had this, if I had that
Oh Jah it's a pity
Drugs using body abusing mind wasting
Nations crumbling, society falls
To Rass to Rass
Our children faced with questions, without answers
Faced with the task of fixing a failing economy
Suffering will be at an all-time high
While others fly on their high
Blocking out reality
Living in pure fantasy
What a bam bam
Young people got it to bear
Blood sweat and tears, open your ears

Crying will be everywhere
As men live in total fear
Drugs using body abusing mind wasting
A new generation without spiritual guidance
Heading in the wrong direction
We need a resurrection
Crime on the rise
Poverty reeks our cities, oh Jah what a pity
Man and man a live so iffy
Youths stay calm
We don't need an uprising, we need to be uplifted
Enlightened and lots of encouragement
We need love for ourselves, we need to show love for others
We owe no one nothing but love
Love from the heart

Take Your Stand

By: Mia Atre & Vernon Paddy

Rise up Black man
Take your stand
Know of our great contribution
Rise up Black woman
Take your stand
You have been nothing but great from the dawn of civilization
From your womb rises great nations
With all your trials all your tribulations
Know of how great you are Black woman
Rise up, rise up Black people
From all corners of this world
Rise up, rise up, know your worth
Rise up, rise up, hold your ground
Heads held high, powerful and proud
Shout and sing praises to the highest King
For we all come from great Queens and Kings
Every struggle, every trial, and every tribulation
Every cross we bore
Remember we all have to burn in our own fire
To become the new, shiny, beautiful you
Rise up Black man
Come up front, never stay in the back
The Creator don't want us to ever be like that
Rise up Black woman
Know your worth
Look in the mirror long and hard
You're perfect, you're beautiful and unique
A rare gem from way back then
Shake off the mental slavery that traps your mind
Realize you're the most expensive of all the wines
That's a fact, Black woman you're the cream of the crop

Terror in Boston

What a cruel intention
What a cruel intention
Man sets off bombs in a Boston marathon
In a Boston marathon
In a Boston marathon
In a Boston marathon
What this teach the nation?
Man have cruel, vicious intentions
Remember Jah control all man
Even their mess up plans
What a mess
What a mess
This is cruelty at its best
People come out to enjoy the fest
Mad man, bad man, you think you got away with this one
Jah Jah a go stop all your future plans to hurt another one
What a mess up revolution
Bomb, what a deadly invention
Terror in Boston
Terror in Boston
Before them fly right
Before them do right
Them a learn how to build bombs
What a dangerous invention
Them a hurt another human
Them a hurt another person
America is a great country
A land of opportunity
They disobey authority
Them a menace to society
What a mess up revolution
Bomb what a deadly invention
Terror in Boston
Terror in Boston

That I Miss

A life filled with bliss
That I miss
A life of care free days filled with fun and laughter
Is a thing of the past
To Rass to Rass
A life with endless possibility
Vigor and youth
Vitality
Dreams yet fulfilled
Pure vision
Fantasy blending with reality
Days into night
Never having to fight
Struggles with neither needs or wants
That I miss
Oh how I miss, oh how I wish
This life wasn't such a bitch
Nine to five plus some
This life is no fun
Money don't walk it run
So we work hard always trying to catch up
Time wait for no man
You either on time or left behind
Everything in life takes money
Money for this, money for that
We quickly abandon our dreams
Our new vision is survival
Our new mission is to stay afloat
Or go down on a sinking boat
Life is a glitch and so-so wish
Life sure is a bitch

The End of The Day

At the end of the day
When the dust settles
The count is taken
Who is right and who is wrong
Who is living and who is gone
At the end of the day
When the bombing
Shooting and looting
Seize
Who get an ease and who was squeeze
No thank you or please
If you know what I mean
At the end of the day
When all is said and done
War is never fun
Such waste of monetary funds
At the end of the day
The results will show
For all to know
It's then up to all of us
To live with the decision
We have made
Can we?
Will we?
The road we have taken
The games we have played
What prayers we have prayed
Did we make the right moves?
Did we step on any one to get to where we're at?
Know the facts
Accept the truth

We're all heading down the same route
From birth to earth
Ashes to ashes
Dust to dust
Our lives is such

The Good Book

You teach us to bow our heads, to be penitent
Never to conquer
When your type search, seek, find, capture
rename claim for Queen and country
For your God and selves
You teach us your laws, set by your elders
Set to suit your kind, not my kind
Not mankind
Your new religion light and white
it set to frighten not enlighten
Your elders white wash the truth
cover, cover up the rights
so you all can feel superior
Knowing our true heritage, our true lineage, our culture
Was far superior, super grand
We were Kings and Queens from many different lands of Africa
Educators, builders, teachers, preachers, philosophers
Warriors, healers, musicians, athletes, leaders
We knew self-worth
We were held in high esteem
You carry us away in captivity yet required from us a song
Our blood, sweat, tears and our lives
You crisscross the blood lines
Now this new generation is loss
They can't seem to fine self-worth
We are faced with this identity crisis
An inferior complex
We are brain washed with the White man's crap
Hollywood life style is the biggest trap
Our elders back wore the stripes of the whip
Momma's broad hips and beautiful lips
Tell me to Rass how could Master ever resist?

Now we got the new mix
Society need a fix
History lean, it bend, it will never be the black man's friend
We people of all beautiful colors
need to come together as one
to build up this new world
that is still so filled with prejudice and hate
To live out our day without fear of being brutalized
To enjoy earthly peace before enjoying perfect peace

The Justice Shit-tem Fail

The justice system fail, the justice shit-tem fail
How the Rass him get bail?
You drink and drive, pray fe no get ketch
Babylon will lock you in jail
The justice system fail, the justice shit-tem fail
How the Rass him get bail?
You smoke a joint a hold a meditate, pray fe no get ketch
Babylon will lock you in jail
The justice system fail, the justice shit-tem fail
How the Rass him get bail?
You cuss two bad words expressing your anger
Pray Babylon don't hear
You will get lock up in jail
The justice system fail, the justice shit-tem fail
How the Rass him get bail?
Watch the brute, watch the brute
Look pon the wicked Rass fool
Kill an innocent
African American youth
The justice system fail, the justice shit-tem fail
How the Rass him get bail?
You a defend your rights
Pop off two shot of warning
Pick up two years for that
Is it because she was African American
BLACK
The justice system fail, the justice shit-tem fail
Is plenty people it fail
Too many to mention
A last week my brother got detention for speaking his mind
They want us to walk and blind
Hear but act deaf

I just heard the news, another innocent brother just got abused
The justice system fail, the justice shit-tem fail
It fail, it fail, and it fail
It fail we the people
You know the type
Right

The Little Rock

These days you better be political correct
You better walk good watch your steps
Careful what you speak
Your neighbors might get upset
You don't see we living in times of
Black and White, wrong and right
Truth v.s. lies
Media propaganda
Hush hush and cover ups, one hand wash the other
These days you better be socially aware
A so-so internet creepiness
Freedom to speak
Powerful people still control the weak
Corruption in every level of government
From the bottom to the top
As long as I'm getting mentality
The see and blind, hear and act deaf mentality
The sellout of our resources, the new colonizing
Foreign investment with personal benefits
Very soon we'll be living on reservations
Our little rock share up like pizza slices
China man, Indian man, Mexicans, Europeans
What's leave for the Black Man?
What's leave for the Jamaicans?
We little rock share up, we little rock tear up, we little rock mash up
Greed and get rich schemes
Scammers, top shooters, dons, party leaders
Teachers and preachers
We little rock share up, we little rock tear up, we little rock sell up
What the hell is up with that?
What's leave for the poor man?
We sell out our heroes

We sell out pride
We sell out our dignity
So we sell the truth
So we sell lies
A how some of you sleep at night
Bank book fat
Mansion splash
Belly full
Security tight
You're on top, tip top
When you fall from grace due to how you sell out your own race
Remember the rich and the poor get buried under the same earth
Man remember thy worth

The Man in Me

The man in me, the man in me
will never give up
will not let negative sounds get me down
The man in me, the man in me
will never sit idle
will not let the ups and downs of life
dull the inner spirit
The man in me, the man in me
Is programed to survive
The inner warrior will surface to defend any fight
The man in me, the man in me
is filled with pure fire
A drive to enjoy life
Eyes that see injustice toward others
A mouth that speaks quickly, openly for equal rights
The man in me, the man in me
is on fire
Blazing hot
no mute or pause
The inner warrior never sleeps
there is help needed for the weak
A voice that must speak
The wicked never sleep
scheming and planning how to cheat from the poor and meek
Our brothers and sisters are dying daily in the streets
Every life matters
No human deserves to die by the hands of those who wear
the uniform of brutality
The man in me, the man in me
is very proud
I'm a blend of every color
I defend truth and rights

Crime and violence knows no color, has no preference
it affects every gender
All human race
Remember it's the human behind the weapon
His or her dark thoughts
controlling their inner man/woman
The man in me, the man in me
knows no fear
The man in me will always care
Praising Jah for the rest of my days

The One Voice

The one voice
Rooted deep within I from creation
Jah who gave I the wise knowledge
To fully under and over stand the truth
Rasta truth
Jah who opened up my eyes to see
This pure light
Rasta light
I never stop speaking for truth and rights
I am representing Rasta
A child of the high king
This battle I must win
For on my side is the highest king
The one voice
Rooted deep within I from creation
Coming from the Mother land Africa
Its super spiritual, it's most natural
It must pour forth
It must flow
The whole world will one day know of Rasta
Rasta greatness
Prophecy reveal, we saw the Ras king from the east
Marcus Garvey the prophet spoke loud and clear
About the black proud might race
To rise up, rise up, rise up
To know who we are, where we came from
United we stand, divided we shall scatter and fall
The different branches of Rasta
Standing tall, strong and will always grow
Fruits of righteousness

All branch of Rasta share the foundation
Root of Jah Rastafari
Alpha and Omega
The beginning and the end
Jah is three person
Blessed Trinity

The Time is Now

America the time is now!
America show we!
Show we you can change
Years of racial war
Blacks, Whites wear the scars
Too many cops abuse their powers
There are families planning funerals
Their sons and daughters dead
America your hands are red, red, blood stain red
Corruption in every level
A quick pat on their hands
Congratulation you have done a great job
Making America great again
Hell no!
We were never great
America is made up of two type
The hunter and the prey
Churches filled with people praying
Praying because they fear
Death by the hands of a fellow citizen
There are those who hate and discriminate
They wouldn't hesitate to make you LATE
America the time is now!
America show us!
Show us you can change
We need swift justice for those who show such hate
Such abuse of their powers
We the tax payers
We the voters
We are counting on you America

They Bring It with Them

They bring it with them come to America
They bring it with them come to America
They bring greed with them
They bring it with them come to America
They bring it with them come to America
They bring prejudice with them
They bring it come to America in their hearts
Hate and envy
Pass it down to their generation
This racial thing a come from far
They bring it with them come to America
They bring it with them come to America
They bring violence with them
They bring it with them come to America
They bring it with them come to America
They bring fever and diseases
They bring it come to America in their hearts
They bring a broken system come implement here
A system they knew was never going to be fair
They bring it with them come to America
They bring it with them come to America
They bring old colonial laws and rules with them
They bring it come to America in their hearts
Hate and envy
Pass it down to their generation
This racial thing a come from far

Thing Set A Way

The thing set a way, the thing set a way
Oh! The thing set a way, oh! Jah, the thing set a way
Things and time dread, earth a run red
Nuff blood a shed, these youths are bold, their hearts are so cold
The thing set a way, the thing set a way
Oh! The thing set a way, oh! Jah, the thing set a way
Rise and fall of government, wars and rumors of war
Corrupt politicians, false preachers, wages the new day slavery
The many haves, the majority of have nots
Greed and get rich schemes
The everyday exodus, movement of Jah's children
Prophesy fulfilling
The thing set a way, the thing set a way
Oh! The thing set a way, oh Jah, the thing set a way
White wash history
It's a mystery how them fool the mass of us
Their teachings and preachings, still got a hold on some of us
So many are still sleeping after four hundred years
The chains and shackles have been removed
Its been replaced with Hollywood life style
Glitter and glamour following a hype
The many who are still trap in mental slavery
The many lost souls, identity crisis
Not truly knowing where we came from, who we are, where we belong
Have wreak years of blood shed
Brothers killing their brothers, such hate for each other
Due to lack of knowledge of self
So many pay a high price for their crisscross blood lines
Society and their color lines, prejudice truly exists
We got to realize the whole world mix
Mix up, mix up, moods and attitudes
The thing set a way, the thing set a way

Oh! The thing set a way, oh! Jah, the thing set a way
Wolfs in sheep clothing, friends who are truly your enemy
World leaders seeking our vote
Check them out they are just a joke
Don't believe their stories
Their generation messed up history
Re-educate your minds, seek and you will find the truth
We have been living years of lies
Know your own story
Dig deep you will get to the real history
Respect self, respect others
For the thing set a way
The thing set a way, the thing set a way
Oh! The thing set a way, oh Jah, the thing set a way

This Girl

Girl you pass me like a hurricane
Your beauty blows my brain
Girl you pass me like a hurricane
My day start calm, the sky was clear
Now it's all blue because I'm thinking of you
Girl you pass me like a hurricane
My life was balanced and calm
Now it's just pure turbulence going on
Pure wind and rain, my heart is in pain
You leave me in aches and pain
Girl you pass me like a hurricane
Your beauty reign, you radiate giving off a heat
You hot from head to feet, you're confident in your style
Don't move so fast bad mama, linger for awhile
I stare at you with mouth open wide
My heart is beating faster, my blood pressure is getting high
I can't lie, for a woman like you I would die
Girl you pass me like a hurricane
Your beauty makes me shiver, my heart skips a beat
Girl you sweet, girl you sweet
You got me fantasizing, you consume my thoughts, I feel paralyzed
Can't speak, can't move, I'm froze yet aroused
Girl you pass me like a hurricane
Your beauty captivates me
Your beauty fascinates me, I feel hypnotized, I'm under your spell
Awake me and take me to your paradise
Let me live in pure happiness and joy
Loving you today and every day after
You can always be the hurricane
I'll make you control me
Just as long as you blow me, just make sure you hold me
I'll go anywhere with you

I'll be the man you want, then some
I promise every day will be lots of fun
Girl you pass me like a hurricane
Your beauty got me going insane
Your beauty have me on a natural high
If you fly, I'll fly up to the sky
I'm so mesmerized by your beauty
As a man I'll perform my duty
The loving won't be short, the loving will be strong
The loving will last the whole night long
Remember you're dealing with a Jamaican
Girl you pass me like a hurricane, girl you pass me like a hurricane
Blow pretty mama, blow, blow pretty mama blow
Just make sure you pass my way again

This Living

Don't let money be the deciding factor
in how you live your life here on Earth
Know your worth
Respect Mother Nature
Appreciate Father Time
This living is a one-time thing
there is no repeat
no do over
Keep clean hands, a pure heart
Love and happiness
should always be in your thoughts
The Earth has a vast amount of riches
Live wise not otherwise
Enjoy Earth to the max
You're born, you live and you will surly die
that's a fact
Don't be too exact
learn to lean and bend
you'll have more friends
Laugh every chance you get
Smile give your face a rest
How do you rate yourself?
Good, better or the best
You ever take stack, wonder or ponder
if you'll only get today, or enjoy some of tomorrow
Only take when in need
Live humble, if you stub your toes and fall
rise up, rise up, and rise up
Give a hand every chance you get

Live with happiness and joy
It's better than pain and sorrow
What is gone is gone and you can't get it back
don't live in the past move forward to Rass to Rass
Leave alone those old sores
There will be new wounds to mend
Yesterday's woes should not be today's sorrow

Thursday Morning

If I could turn back the hands of time
I would for you
To shield you from this pain
To cover you from any harm or shame
Remember that's what a brother is here for
When you cry I'll cry too
When you're down I'll be down too
I'll hold your hands
You can lean on my shoulders
I'll help to bring back fun and laughter
Remember that's what a brother is here for
Just so you know I feel your pain
I love you with every drop of blood that runs through my veins
I'll never judge you
Never look down upon you
What I'll do is remind you of Jah's love
The sweet life in the here after
Remember that's what a brother is here for
Forgiveness is divine
Salvation is free
Jah loves you my sister
I'll remind you to keep humble thoughts
It's the food that will feed the heart
I'll remind you that Jah and you shall never part
So long as you keep him in your heart
Hold your head up
You're a child of the king on high
Forgiveness is divine
Salvation is free
Jah loves you and me
Anything you need you only have to ask
I'll give my every, I'll give my last

Remember that's what a brother is here for
It's a pity others can't see what I see in you
Only if they could, they'll see the true inner beauty you possess
The countless good deeds you have done
Your hands have stretched across this land
Helping others in their time of distress
You deserve only the best, pure fun and laughter
Never a day of disaster

Air & Time

By: Mia Atre & Vernon Paddy

Time, time, time, oh how I love you
Even a mere second is precious
A day what a blessings
A week ever so grand
I am living, my heart is ticking
With sweet time, time, time
Time, time, time, oh how I adore you
To see a New Year words can't express
This happiness
The new memories made
The ones shared
Oh for every second of time I do care
I do appreciate
I'm living, my heart ticking
With sweet time, time, time
Time, time, time, oh how I need you
Every second, every minute, every hour
Every day I celebrate
I'm jubilant, I'm excited
Air and time we can't exist without them
Without air or time our lives would end
Is it fair then to say
Air and time are our best friends
I'm living, my heart is ticking
With sweet time, time, time

Jah Only

All praise and glory
To Jah only
All that I got is Jah give I that
The clothes on my back
The food in my pots
I give thanks and praise for that
All praise and glory
To Jah only
Jah's love flows through my heart
Like a river pure and clear
It's Jah only that I fear
With Jah you never have to worry or fret
He lead the blind, he direct the deaf
He heal and resurrect
He'll mold and make you a new
The teachings of Jah is pure truth
Respect Mother Nature
Love Father Time
Jah see and know all men's vibes
We're all a ticking clock
That one day has to stop
Respect oneself
Respect others
Keep clean hands, a pure heart
You and Jah will never part

Travelling Through Babylon

So long I'm travelling through Babylon
So long I'm travelling through Babylon
So long I'm travelling through Babylon
I have to watch out for my enemies
I got to protect my head
Many want to see Rasta dead
The broken system
Dread, dread, dread
The broken system
Red, red, red
Rasta don't bow, Rasta don't beg
So long I'm travelling through Babylon
So long I'm travelling through Babylon
So long I'm travelling through Babylon
I have to be careful with my steps
They done have their traps set
Rasta don't eat at their table
Rasta don't able
Rasta don't able
We no longer have to sing and dance for our supper
A Jah we praise everyday
So long I'm travelling through Babylon
So long I'm travelling through Babylon
So long I'm travelling through Babylon
My crown represent the highest
My lifestyle shows love and respect
A Jah-Jah I praise
I praise him night and day
So long I'm travelling through Babylon
So long I'm travelling through Babylon
So long I'm travelling through Babylon

Trouble Free

Years of life together trouble free
One day gosh your troubles are plenty
No cash a flow Jah know
My rent need to be payed, soon you can't stay
Cash in hand you spend it one by one
No food to eat, no energy to beat the mean streets
You talking to the man in the mirror
Hoping for a change, for better not worst
To have money in my purse
You never wish for you and your woman a curse
Things getting from bad to worst
Right now all I can think about is this thirst
Funny how the mind works
I've been living for days on my inner reserve
Food is a thing of the past, two to three days to be exact
I can't remember the last time I crap
My woman been walking the street in the heat
looking for some day work
Each day is the same old story, rain a fall but the dirt tough
Pot a cook but the food not enough
My friends all said they would come around
I saw them drive pass me on my way into town
No one bother to stop, I guess I smell bad and look like crap
Someone told me about a job in the next town over
Guess I should just gas up my Jeep or Land Rover, and drive on over
Right now I'm living in hope and might die in Constance Springs
Poverty got me a way, my mind is weary and it strays
Drifting in and out of sanity
It's hard to reason when you're this hungry
A hungry man is truly an angry man
I'm mad with and at the world
Have you ever had to look your kids in their eyes?

Send them away to their Granny
Telling them to hold tight, things going to be all right
Well let me tell you all I told a straight up lie
I do miss little Geneva and Clive
I do see my woman from a distance coming
Oh Jah let there be good news tonight, let
me praise your name upon high
Let poverty be dead to the I
Let poverty leave the I and the I
Oh Jah no later than this day or tomorrow
give me a brighter day I'm tired to live in sorrows
I'm tired to walk and sell two-two bottles
I am tired to see my woman face filled with sorrows
No one should have to live this poor when some have it galore
I had to sell my furniture we now sleep on the floor
There is a few neighbors down the road that's equally as poor
saw them in Church last night singing and clapping
Maybe I'll join them tonight if my situation is right
Oh Jah let me see some light
I must leave out of this darkness
Again let poverty be dead tonight

Forward Ever

Step up front
Never in the back
Jah know we no play that
Forward ever backward never
Lead we come to lead
With clean hands and pure hearts
For Jah and I will never part
Forward ever backward never
I come to dwell in love and unity
Spreading a positive message
So lend a listening ear and have no fear
Jah is always near
Forward ever backward never
If we spread love and come together in oneness
We can overthrow evil
Stop poverty in its tracks
Forward ever backward never
I come to seek equal rights and justice
For all levels of society
Settling for only the highest level of education
For our kids
Teaching the old ways
Oral and written traditions
Rewriting history
Our religions
The cultures of mother land Africa
Too many lost souls
It's time we truly know
Who we are and where we came from
Then and only then we can move forward
FORWARD EVER BACKWARD NEVER

Valley of Decisions

Though I walk in the valley of decision
I stand firm in Jah-Jah
That's my only mission
Make up your mind
Love Jah-Jah, love Jah-Jah
Oh! Jah I adore
Oh! Jah I adore
Jah open all doors
Jah is ever sure
Though I walk in the valley of decision
I stand firm in Jah-Jah
That's my only mission
Make up your mind
Love Jah-Jah, love Jah-Jah
Oh! Jah I adore
Oh! Jah I adore
Keep Jah on your side
With you he will abide
Though I walk in the valley of decision
I stand firm in Jah-Jah
That's my only mission
He paid the admission
I better accept, never reject
With Jah you get the best

Voices

By: Mia Atre & Vernon Paddy

Careful of the voices in your head
Some could be from the living
Some from the dead
Being depressed, being stressed is dread
It gets harder to separate reality from fantasy
Lately I have been speaking more to the dead
My mind takes me beyond, my mind takes me back
I relive the past
To Rass, to Rass, to Rass, to Rass
Careful of the voices you let into your mind
Some will pass through
Some will linger for awhile
Playing tricks on your mind
Some voice will enlighten
Some voice will frighten you
My mind goes in and out with time
I see things to come, I see things I've done
It scares me to know
I live in this fantasy land
Where fools plan, wish and hope
You all think it's a joke
These voices just poked
They leave messages too
The reality and the fantasy all blends together
It's becoming one big ball of madness
Oh Rass, oh Rass, oh Rass what a mess
What a Rass mess, my mind is perplexed
Confused, over worked, used and abused
Careful of the voices
Careful of what you speak

Careful of what you'll become
The story just start, the story has no end
This story tell truth, this story tell lies
Just wait the voices will tell me what to say
Oh crap I'm out of minutes
Only text, I can text
Oh crap my mind vex
These voices don't take checks
You better have cash in hand
Or walk up and down like a mad man
This story just start, this story has no end
So till next time
When there are voices in my head

Walk in The Light

Walk into the light
Knowing Jah is the light
With Jah in your heart, all things get right
There is a balance with oneself and Mother Nature
You're now more appreciative of Father's Time
Knowing Jah is the light
Walk into the light
A child of Jah, a child of light
Jah is the main light, the giver of life
Walk in the light and shine bright
Speak only truth and rights
Child of light, child of Jah
Walk in Jah path, with clean hands and a pure heart
Child of Jah, child of light
Walk into the light
Accepting Jah as your source of light
You and Jah shall never part
As long as Jah is the one in your heart
Walk in the light and shine bright
Child of Jah, child of light
Jah is the main light, the giver of life

War Plans

The war had a plan
Design by man
For a financial gain
A commodity
We'll trade
The war have its gain
Sometime it's all in vain
Every war have its cost and causes
Some so lost
The war have a price of human sacrifice
Of human cries
Of human lives
Of blood, sweat and tears
Others left in despair
Abandoned
Forsaken
Unforgiven
All in the cost of war
To Rass to Rass
Can we afford this high price?
Just to toss away human lives
To Rass to Rass
Can we afford such a sacrifice?
These young beautiful lives
To fulfill man's war plans

We Come a Long Way

We come a long way so let us not pretend
Modern technology has become human's best friend
We're all living on earth so let's respect life
Remember when traveling overseas was really done on seas
Remember when only the big cities had electric light
Remember when only a chosen few had telephones
Remember when television was only in black and white
And shut off at mid night
Remember when a only pit toilet and chamber pot
And man have to pop a squat
We come a long ways from days when
Transportation wasn't so grand
And infrastructure wasn't so strong
Medicine was in testing stages and humans was used as lab rats
We come a long ways from days when
Agriculture wasn't so advance
Man have always had the earth, soil, and plants
But knew not how to reproduce, maintain, to export
In mass production
We come a long ways from days when
Politics was a one man show
Now the nation have a voice a say in how we like to be governed
We come a long ways from days when
Fashion and style lack creativity
Now fashion and style is a multimillion empire
With more creativity to satisfy each and every one
We come a long ways from days when
We use to live in huts and one level flats
Now man build skyscrapers, bridges across rivers and water
Man build tunnels under cities and streets
Knowledge from Jah in man has increased

We Have Come a Long Way

We come a long way so let us not pretend
Modern technology has become human
Best friends
We are all living on earth so let's respect life
Respect for man respect for woman
Respect for husband respect for wife
Respect for our children a them hold the future in their hands
We come a long way so let us not pretend
Modern technology has become human
Best friends
We are all living on earth so let's respect life
Respect our selves
Respect for others
Respect to all teachers
Who a pass on knowledge
Let's make sure our youths all go a college
Respect for our elders
For our fore parents who all pass
They pave the way toiled and fought
For equal right and justice
We come a long way so let us not pretend
Modern technology has become human
Best friends
We are living on earth so let's respect life
Make us talk about old history
We need to rewrite that old crap
Too much of it lean
We have to get it straight
Wait, wait
We have to deal with them one by one
Start from the bottom a go straight up a top
Not calling any names

For they know themselves
For far too long
Our little country have been raped
We're tired to watch the rich get richer
And the poor stay poor
Jah know
We come along way so lets us not pretend
Modern technology has become human
Best friends
We are all living on earth so let's respect life

What The Mother

By: Mia Atre & Vernon Paddy

What the mother ---- she was thinking
Got the little gal into
Heavy liquor drinking
What this mother was thinking
What this mother was thinking
What the mother ---- she was thinking
Got the little boy into
Ganja smoking, drugs smuggling
What this mother was thinking
What this mother was thinking
What the mother ---- she was thinking
Got the little gal into
Prostituting, body selling and child pornography
What this mother was thinking
What this mother was thinking
What the mother ---- she was thinking
Got the youths into
Drive by shooting, gun slinging, and vigilante style killing
What this mother was thinking
What this mother was thinking
What the mother ---- she was thinking
Got the little child into
Snatch and grab looting, stealing and scheming
What this mother was thinking
What this mother was thinking
What the mother ---- she was thinking
Got her kids into
Earth polluting, trash dumping, nothing constructive
What this mother was thinking
What this mother was thinking

What the mother ---- she was thinking
Got her son and daughter into
Crime spree, now their faces all over the TV
To hell with a mother like she
No human forgiveness for thee
She better start praying to the Almighty
If this is what she a teach
I guess she practice what she preach
What this mother was thinking
What this mother was thinking

Which Direction

Which direction this country a take
Which direction this country a take
Some say right, some say left
Some say up, some say down
We sure don't want to be led by a clown
Which direction this country a take
Which direction this country a take
Some say forward, some say backwards
Some say into the future, some say into the past
That can't be good to Rass to Rass
Which direction this country a take
Which direction this country a take
Some say for better, some say for worst
So many are quiet, so many are verbal
Some say win, lose or draw
We all will be screwed to Rass to Rass
Which direction this country a take
Which direction this country a take
A beg you all get it right before it's too late
We might all have to migrate back a yard
As they say no where no better than yard
Me a go call Becky find out what's going on a yard
See which direction the new man a take
Before me jump out of frying pan into fire

Who Am I

Who am I to not worship the Creator?
Who am I to not worship the Father?
Where would I be in the hereafter?
It's good to worship Jah-Jah
Who am I to not accept the Creator?
There is no other greater
Praises I give now, praises I give later
Securing my hereafter
Forgiveness is divine
I praise up Jah-Jah all the time
Mercy and grace showed to me
All my praises are unto thee
Who am I to not worship Jah-Jah?
Who am I to not worship the Mighty Father?
Where would I be in the hereafter?
It's grand to worship Jah-Jah
Who am I to not accept Jah-Jah?
There is no other greater than Jah-Jah
All praises I give, all praises I give
Jah-Jah the Highest King
The most high King
His salvation allow I to win
New lights I see, new mind set
Grace and mercies is for all to get
Place Jah-Jah up front you'll never regret
Re-educate your mind, seek and you shall find
Peace is within every one
With Jah-Jah you'll have the balance
With Jah-Jah you have the formula
to live here on Earth and in the hereafter
Jah-Jah is the Creator
Jah-Jah is the Mighty Father

It's glorious to worship Jah-Jah
Who am I to not accept Jah-Jah?
Now I see the light I'm going to shine ever bright
A new child of the Highest King
The Highest King
My days are fulfilled, new praises I sing
I'm full joyed, my life ever bless, nothing is lacking
With Jah-Jah a so the thing set
A so the thing set, a so the thing set
Jah-Jah is simple the best
Come one come all come
Come follow Jah-Jah
A new child of the Highest King
The highest, the highest king

With You When You're Right

I see you my brother
I'm with you when you're right
I saw you giving off warning
I heard when you gave of sound
I see you've awoke
You see it's no joke in these streets
You're legit and I hope you never quit
I see you my sister
I hear you loud and clear
I understand your concerns, I understand your fears
I love that you're over protective of your youths
I like your cause, it's a good fight
I'm with you when you're right
I see you my brother
I will stand by your side, I will march with you
I will pick up arms and fight
Too long we've been suffering
We face the same fights
Your win is my win, your loss is my loss
It's a heavy cross to carry
We must forge ahead without fears
I see you my sister, in all your glory
You only want equality
You only want your share
I see you my sister, in all your hallelujah
Your years of suffering was never fair
When no one acted like they cared
You stood the test of time
Bounced back from all hardship
You wear the scars of the whip
You carry their offspring on your hips
With your head held high like magic you rise

You possess what they desire
Inner beauty and grace a quality so rare
You possess what they desire
Inner fire; it's like heaven on earth between your thighs
I see you my sister, perfect in everyway
I see you my brother, never stop
Keep raising your family
Keep being the king of your kingdom
Keep your head held high, eyes on the prize
I'm with you when you're right
I see you my sister, never stop
Keep holding it down
Keep being the queen you were born to be
Keep your head held high, you are all our prize

Woman

Men respect woman, men respect woman
All woman
Every woman
Its inner divine for only they can bring forth a child
Men respect woman, men respect woman
All woman
Every woman
Jah creation can't be denied, men still to this day
marvel at the wonder of Mother and Child
Men respect woman, men respect woman
All woman
Every woman
Remember you came from a woman
It was woman who kept us all safe inside
cared for us as infants and child
Men we grew up and still need woman to be by our sides
to be our equals
to love till the day we die

Yea Though

Yea though I walk through the valley of the shadows of death
As a child of the Highest King
Jah will protect my every steps
Protect my every steps
Protect my every steps
Yea though I walk through the valley of the shadows of death
As a child of the Highest King
My love for Jah
It seal and set
It allow me to never forget
A Jah guide and direct
A Jah guide and direct
Yea though I walk through the valley of the shadows of death
As a child of the Highest King
I see how the thing set
I see how the thing set
I'm grateful for this new mind set
Rasta light a reflect
I know I'm ever bless
Ever bless
Ever bless
Yea though I walk through the valley of the shadows of death
Every King need an Empress
Each molding the next to reach and achieving only the best
King men show love and total respect to every Empress
King men most important be faithful to your Empress

You and I

You and I collide
For the very last time
It's a hit and miss
Your mind too mixed
Your emotions on high
Your heart been broken
It never seem you got it fixed
So I pay the price
You quick to dish out a verbal lashing
You blame me for this or that
Before finding out the facts
You never seem to be happy or ever satisfy
Always complaining
Crying about this or that
Financial Knick and knacks
That where your heart at
You and I collide
For the very last time
It's a hit and miss
Your mind too mixed
You fix up the outer
You sure look fine
Your inner could use some thinner
To wash away the thick layer of crud and mud
Love and hate, fire and ice
Oh what a waste
Your words are deep
I wonder how you sleep
When you dish out the dirt
I wonder if you see your own worth
You and I collide
For the very last time

It's a hit and miss
Your mind too mixed
I leave feeling like a winner
I'm glad I didn't eat your dirty dinner
You fix up the outer
When you should've worked on the inner
You could've been such a winner
Instead of being an abuser and user
Your house of cards will crumble
I wish you were more humble
Watch your steps you're going to stumble

You Ever Wonder

You ever wonder why bad things happen to good people?
You ever wonder, you ever wonder, you ever wonder
Why the good die young?
Seven times rise, seven times fall
One step forward and two steps back
All man to understand that
No matter what, Jah got your back
No hollering, no screaming, no stress
Not going to change destiny
As it's written so shall it be
Live your live stress free
Learn to let go
Our loved ones die as we go through life
No feel no way
All man journey shall fade away
All man born, live and die
You every wonder why
they crucify Jesus Christ?
Sell out Marcus for rice?
Kill Martin Luther for telling truth and showing people the rights?
You ever wonder, you ever wonder, you ever wonder
A set of guys invade
Rip, rape, rob and enslave another
For their own gratification and financial gain
and get away for years
You ever wonder, you ever wonder, you ever wonder
how some men allow the Devil to come inside?
To corrupt their every thoughts
Lead them in a path of self-destruction
How the hearts of men get cold
Rob from the sick and the old
Hurting their fellow humans along the way

You ever wonder, you ever wonder, you ever wonder
Men create the laws
then act surprised when men break them
No crime under the sun is new
Nations have been fighting nations
Wars, rumors of wars
Prejudice against another will never seize
Hate exist understand this
Love conquers all
Jah is greater than man
Only the meek shall inherit the earth
Blessed are those hungry and thirsty for righteousness
Bless is a peace maker

Your Inner Warrior

Try a little harder my brothers
Try a little harder my sisters
Never give up
Dig deep within
You will find you're a warrior
you will see you got what it takes
to rise up stronger every time
that you are discriminated against
Persecuted for your beliefs
Wrongly accused
Looked down upon for your beautiful uniqueness
When words used against you are so painful
You will see you got what it takes
to find your inner warrior
Remember brothers and sisters you are from Kings and Queens
An original masterpiece
you're truly unique from head to feet
You're not white washed or watered down
straight out of Africa your heritage can be found
We are all branches from that main root
Mother Africa
Four hundred years plus and they're still fighting against us
They took us away from paradise
In this land we now call home and we have all the rights to do so
The many greats that found their inner warrior
stood up tall, refused to be broken any more, fought back
suffered, cried, and died in this Country America
the land of the free and home of the brave
Oh! Never let us forget the slaves

Try a little harder my brothers
Try a little harder my sisters
Never give up
Dig deep within
you will find you're a warrior
you will see you got what it takes
to rise up stronger every time

Your Own Story

This is my story
This is not a song
White people captured us out of Africa
Take us to these faraway lands
Write their history to them it was a victory
To us colored people a horror story
Put us to work without pay on their plantations
Brain wash us
Force religion
Whip us when they felt like
Rape our wives, sisters and mothers
to build up their work force population
Tell me if this wasn't wrong
This is my story
This is not a song
White people captured us out of Africa
Take us to these faraway lands
This start slavery in these parts of the world
Slavery wasn't new, it existed even within Africa
The different tribes and clans enslave one another
Beautiful colored people find your own stories
Their history lean it bend
It can never be your friend
It set to suit only them
Live by faith and follow your destiny
Respect yourself, respect others
Create your own story
Dig deep within
Reeducate oneself

Respect your lineage
Respect your race
Respect your culture
Respect your heritage
Seek peace from within, seek peace from within
Know you have a soul
Write your own story
Create your own history

You're My Fix

You're my fix
You're my fix
You're the answer to all this
You're an angel sent
My heart, mind and soul is renewed
Oh! It's all because of you
My life has a new meaning
Oh how I enjoy our talks and reasoning
I now have reasons to smile again
You are heaven sent
You're my fix
You're my fix
You're the answer to all this
Oh! How I adore thee
My love for you will live till the day I die
Since we reconnect
I can't lie I feel extra bless
The time and space apart created our individual unique stories
I now pray, let's create together a beautiful love story
Blending our past with the present
Take a leap of faith
For you I don't want to wait
You're my fix
You're my fix

Printed in the United States
by Baker & Taylor Publisher Services